King Edward VII School

A Centenary Celebration

Michael Walker

First published in Great Britain in 2005 by
The Book Guild, Lewis, East Sussex

This revised edition was produced in 2019 by
K.E.S.Publications
King Edward Vll School
Gaywood Road
King's Lynn
PE30 2QB

Typeset in Times and printed by DSD Colour Printers,
King's Lynn.

A catalogue record for this book is available from the British Library.

ISBN number: 978-0-9565697-4-5

Contents

Introduction to the 2005 Edition

The aim of this book is to trace the development of King Edward Vll School from 1510, the earliest known date for its origin, and to provide a record which celebrates the school's success at different periods in its history. In the main I have concentrated on the period from the end of the nineteenth century, because the school as we know it today emerged at that time. The name was changed to King Edward Vll Grammar School in 1903 and the school was moved to its present site, into the magnificent new buildings donated by Sir William Lancaster, in 1906.

The first chapter traces the development of the school from its original foundation to 1887, covering its time in the Charnel Chapel at St. Margaret's Church, the move to the Butchers' Shambles on Saturday Market Place and then to the School Master's House in St. James Street. 1887 is seen as a critical date because it marks the appointment of the Head Master who was to take the school from the old building in St. James Street to the new Gaywood Road site. Chapters 2 to 7 examine the nature of the school under successive Heads. The information included covers factual information such as numbers on roll and results in examinations, the range of extra-curricular activities provided, particularly significant or controversial issues, the contribution of staff and students to the school's success, changes in the buildings, and links to the royal family.

The main sources of information have been documents in the Borough Archives such as the Corporation Hall Books, together with Minutes of Governors' Meetings, correspondence, copies of *The Lennensian* (the school magazine), HMI and OFSTED inspection reports, early written accounts of the school, individual contributions by old pupils and ex-members of staff and other miscellaneous sources. Inevitably the nature of the final chapter which covers the period when I was Head is somewhat different in that I have written about a period with which I am very familiar and the amount of information available is far greater than for some of the earlier periods.

For students at K.E.S. in more recent years, I should perhaps explain that up to 1979, when the school became comprehensive, old boys were known as Old Lennensians, a name which derives from the fact that, for a time, up to 1903 it was the Lynn Grammar School. The school magazine was known as *The Lennensian* for the same reason.

Michael Walker, 2005.

Introduction to the revised 2019 Edition

This new edition has been changed in a number of ways. Firstly Chapter 1 has been significantly shortened since my second book on the school, *Diary of a Grammar School* (2010), covered the period from 1510 to 1903 in considerable detail. In the final chapter I have added information about the Queen's second visit to the school, in January 2007, and about the rebirth of the Old Lennensians' Association. I have also taken the opportunity to include in most chapters some additional photographs and information.

Since writing the two books about the Lynn Grammar School and King Edward Vll School, I have also published histories of the West Norfolk and King's Lynn High School for Girls, the Alderman Catleugh Schools and the Gaywood Park Schools. The Borough Archive situated in the Old Gaol House building in King's Lynn has a wealth of documentary and photographic material on all these schools. It is open to the public each afternoon from Tuesday to Friday.

Michael Walker, 2019.

Acknowledgements for the 2005 Edition

I wish to express my thanks to all those who have contributed to the book and to those who have helped me in locating sources of information, for which particular thanks go to Sandra Harvey, the highly-efficient secretary to three successive K.E.S. Heads and unofficial keeper of the school records, and to Susan Maddock of the Norfolk Records Office. Thanks also go to David Pitcher, Richard Griffiths and Mike Douglass, who have read sections of the book and made helpful suggestions, and to Steve Jukes, Bob Booth, Dick Goodchild, Paul Marsh (of the *Lynn News*) and Neil Haversham (of the *EDP*) for their help in obtaining copies of particular photographs.

I am grateful to the *Lynn News* and to the *Eastern Daily Press* for permission to reproduce sections from their reports on school events and for a large number of the photographs. These are acknowledged where the source is known but some of the photographs from the school collection could also have originally appeared in the press. Material from the Royal Archives is used by kind permission of Her Majesty Queen Elizabeth ll.

I should also like to take this opportunity to record my appreciation to all the staff, both teaching and non-teaching, who worked with me in the twelve years I was Head and who contributed so much to making the school successful in the last decade of the twentieth century and the early years of the twenty-first century. Especial thanks to six Deputy Heads, Richard Griffiths, John Smallwood, Kate Wadlow, Andy Osborne, Judith Carlisle and Mike Douglass, all of whom gave me invaluable help and support. I am also particularly grateful to Heather Massen, the School Administrator for much of the time I was Head. In addition I wish to put on record the excellent support I received from the Governors, ably led for much of the period by Sylvia Roberts, and from the Clerk and Old Lennensian, Michael Fillenham (1957-63). Finally enormous thanks go to my wife, Elizabeth, for her continuing help and support and for putting up with numerous piles and boxes of information taking up space in so many corners of the house.

I must apologise in advance to those deserving recognition whom I have not mentioned. I have tried to name, in the different eras, those students who were particularly successful at school, either academically or in some other field of activity, or who became so in later life. Inevitably, I will have missed many people who should have been mentioned, not by design, but because the records were not always as complete as I should like them to have been. Similarly, of the hundreds of staff who have worked at the school over the last century I have been able to acknowledge the contribution of relatively few, especially from more recent decades. Again I apologise.

Further acknowledgements

Thanks are due to Bob Booth (1950-58), Brian Gadd (1953-58) and Ian Finbow (1956-62) for some of the new photographs included in this revised edition and also to the *Lynn News* for the photographs of the Queen's visit to the school in January 2007. I am particularly grateful to my wife, Elizabeth, and to Bob Childs (1966-72) for proof reading the revised text and for making helpful suggestions. Many thanks also to Brenda Lance for her skilful work in improving the quality of some of the older photographs. Finally my thanks goes to Dale Thorne at DSD Colour Printers for his skill in setting the text and photographs.

1. The Origins of the Grammar School

Some references can be found to the provision of education in Lynn in the 14th and 15th centuries but the year 1510 has long been taken as the key date when considering the origins of the school. This was the date of the will of a local burgess, Thomas Thoresby, in which there was provision for the upkeep of a priest on condition that he prayed daily for Thomas's soul and taught 'six children in grammar and song.' The income would come from four pieces of pasture in Gaywood.

Sometime between 1538 and 1543 Thomas Thoresby's son, another Thomas, believing that the conditions in his father's will were not being kept, decided to take back the land in Gaywood. However an agreement, dated 1 October 1543, was worked out whereby the four pieces of pasture in Gaywood, referred to in his father's will, would be granted to the Lynn Corporation provided that it appointed a well-qualified priest who would teach six boys in grammar and song and these boys would pray daily for the soul of Thomas Thoresby and others.

Some commentators, such as William Taylor in *Antiquities of Lynn* (1844), believe that, under the Chantries Act of 1548, the lands in Gaywood were confiscated by the Crown, because the conditions attached to the bequest were considered at the time of the Reformation to be superstitious. Under that Act, property bequeathed to pay for the daily chanting of prayers for the dead could be confiscated. William Richards, author of *The History of Lynn* (1812), refers to the school being established by the Lynn Corporation almost immediately after the dissolution of the monasteries, that is in the late 1530s or early 1540s, and, in some private correspondence in 1818, suggests that the land, having been seized by the Crown, was then granted to the Corporation, which felt obliged to apply the income to the original purpose.

Whatever the truth of the situation involving Thomas Thoresby and the land in Gaywood, the unbroken history of the school under the control of the Corporation can be traced from November 1550 when the Borough Hall Book refers to John Rackster 'now being the grammar school master.' He was to receive a salary of £10 per year and 'a chaldron of coals.' The salary was increased to £10.10s in 1553 and a house, rent free, was provided in 1556.

The need for repairs to the School Master's house was regularly reported over the years. As indicated on the stone built into the wall of the 1906 building, the front of the house was rebuilt, in 1658/59, during the mayoralty of Henry Bell, whose son was the architect of the Lynn Custom House. Despite the fact that Edward Bell, the School Master at the time, was the Mayor's brother, he was required to pay one third of the cost of the work. He did however live there for forty-one years, being appointed in 1637 and retiring in 1678. By this stage there was clear evidence that the Corporation accepted complete responsibility for the school, and not just the salary and perquisites of the Master. This was demonstrated in 1659 when it agreed to provide 40 shillings for the purpose of buying books for the Grammar School and again in 1662 when 20 shillings was granted for the same purpose. Very aware of the shortage of books, Edward Bell, on his retirement, presented the Mayor with twenty-six volumes and the Town Clerk was directed to make a catalogue of them to be hung up in the Grammar School together with the donor's name.

The school in the early days was located in the Charnel Chapel, a fourteenth century building attached to St Margaret's Church on what is now Saturday Market Place. Underneath the structure there was an ossuary or charnel-house, wherein the bones taken out of the many graves in the cemetery were deposited. This ceased to be used in 1779/80 and for a period of some forty years

The Charnel Chapel by the Revd. Edward Edwards

the Grammar School was located in one or, for a time, two rooms above the Butchers' Shambles, also on Saturday Market Place. Neither of these buildings would today be considered appropriate locations for a school. Although it had been used for the boarders from quite early in the school's history, the Master's house in St James Street, near the corner with what is today called Tower Street, was not used for teaching until the 1820s.

The Hall Books show that in July 1779 the plans for a new Butchers' Shambles, 'with school rooms above', were approved. It was to be built on the ground where the old grammar school stood, 'or

as close as may be' and the grammar school building was to be taken down. The new Shambles was certainly in use by 1780 when the building was insured for £1000. The exact date when the school was transferred to St James Street is also not absolutely clear. However, in November 1820 the Corporation received a proposal from a group of local men who offered to build two school rooms next to the grammar school playgrounds near St James Street in lieu of the two rooms over the Shambles, which

The Butchers' Shambles on Saturday Market Place, pulled down in 1914

The doorway to the Lynn Grammar School, above which are stones showing the dates of major rebuilding of the School Master's house in 1658/59 and 1825

could then be used as a library or for reading or subscription rooms. The General Purposes Committee of the Corporation examined the plan and the specification of the proposed new building and resolved it 'be erected at the proper season of the next year, upon the plan proposed.' In 1822 there is a reference to repairs of the room in the Saturday Market Place, 'lately occupied by the Revd. Thomas Kidd as a grammar school.' So sometime in 1821 or 1822 the teaching was transferred. In 1825 the Corporation decided to rebuild the School Master's house in St James Street at a cost of £1320. This was marked by a stone set above the door of the school house which read: *Rebuilt 1825 William Swatman Mayor*, along with a second stone recording the rebuilding in 1658/59 and a third stone with the Lynn crest. These stones will be referred to again in later chapters.

The fortunes of the Grammar School saw ups and downs in the eighteenth and nineteenth centuries. However during the headship of the Revd. Dr Thomas White (1858–74), the school became very successful. Interestingly in the information produced for the candidates for the appointment in 1858 it was stated that the school was founded in 1543, the date of the agreement between Thomas Thoresby the younger and the Mayor and Burgesses to grant the lands in Gaywood, as specified in his father's will, if the Corporation employed a School Master.

An advertisement for the school from 1868 lists the Mayor and Corporation as patrons and boasts 'the unusual distinction of a valuable Gold Medal, given annually as a Prize by HRH the Prince of Wales and presented by His Royal Highness in person at Sandringham House.' Further, 'attached to the school are Six Exhibitions to Cambridge, for which Boarders are eligible.' It said that the advantages of the school included excellent dormitories, 'with a separate bed for each boy', a very large playground, a cricket field seven acres in extent and access to sea-water swimming baths. As well as the Head Master and Second Master, two other teachers are listed, including a Foreign Languages Master. The course of Education covered 'Divinity, Classics, Mathematics, the French and German Languages, Elementary Science, English Literature, Grammar and Composition, History and Geography, Arithmetic, Reading, Writing and Drawing.' The fees were 40 guineas for those under 12 and 45 guineas for older boys. There was a reduction for the 'sons of clergymen with small incomes.'

The school in the nineteenth century produced some distinguished alumni, not least Sir William Lancaster who was to become the school's greatest benefactor. Dr George Coulton, a pupil from 1867 to 1871, became a Fellow of St John's College, Cambridge; and Guy Dawber (1871-77) who was awarded the Royal Institute of British Architects Gold Medal in 1928 and was knighted in 1936, served as President of both the Architectural Association and the RIBA.

There is little doubt that the great achievement of the school in the nineteenth century was to secure royal patronage through the award of the Gold Medal. The first award was made to H. Bristow in April 1865 and it is possible that it was intended to be a one-off acknowledgement by Edward, Prince of Wales, of the fact that Lynn Grammar School boys were among the first to greet the white-rose-decked bridal train when it brought the newly-married Prince and Princess of Wales to King's Lynn on the way to Sandringham. In 1866 however the Prince indicated that he intended to award the Gold Medal (of the value of ten guineas) annually and regulations governing the award were drafted by Dr White. It was 'to be offered every other year for classical studies and mathematics, and in alternate years for modern studies, including history, English literature, geography, composition and the French and German languages.' There was to be 'a special examination for the medal conducted by some competent person not connected with the school.' No boy was to be eligible unless he had been at least one year at the school. The intention was also that no boy should win the prize more than once, although A. E. Flaxman did so in 1865/6 and in 1866/7 because he was awarded it for Modern Studies on the first occasion and for Classics and Mathematics on the second.

Normally the Gold Medal was presented personally by the Prince of Wales at Sandringham House but there were three exceptions. The first was on 7 July 1869 when he and Princess Alexandra visited the Lynn Grammar School in St. James Street, the same day as the official opening of the Alexandra Dock. The school obviously broke up for the summer holidays rather earlier than today. Dr White, wrote to parents at the end of May telling them of the visit and informing them that the summer holidays would therefore have to be postponed for three weeks. The fees would be increased. According to the report in the *Lynn Advertiser* the visit almost descended into farce, since a note was delivered to the Head Master at about 4 o'clock, saying that the Prince would perform the opening ceremony at the Docks before visiting the school. When this was announced some of the 200 guests began to leave. However the Royal party arrived almost immediately. During his visit the Prince of Wales presented his Gold Medal to A. B. Howard of Long Sutton. His Royal Highness made reference to the fact that on former occasions he had presented the medal privately at Sandringham but he thought it might give more pleasure for Howard to receive it among his schoolfellows. He said, 'I hope that this medal will contribute to your success in future life and that it may be a stimulus to you for further exertions.'

An unusual Gold Medal presentation took place in June 1872. The Norfolk Agricultural Show was held that year in Lynn and so the Prince of Wales received the winner and Dr White in his tent at the show. The medallist on that occasion was R. L. Collier. The third occasion when Edward presented the Gold Medal other than at Sandringham was at the Official Opening of King Edward Vll Grammar School on 5 November 1906, of which more will be said in the next chapter.

The Prince of Wales Gold Medal for 1880/81

As far as is known none of the original medals awarded by the Prince of Wales survives. One of them, awarded to George Mossop, the winner in 1880/81, was returned to the school in 1945 and for many years was displayed in a glass cabinet in the Hall. Unfortunately, along with all the silver cups it was stolen on 23 October 1980. However we do know what the medal looked like as a photograph appeared in *The Lennensian* in 1965 as part of an article celebrating the award of the hundredth Gold Medal.

When Dr White left in 1874 to take up a living at Hambledon in Hampshire he was presented, on behalf of the pupils, past and present, with 'a handsome timepiece in ornamental marble' and Mrs White with 'an elegant chased silver tea tray.' The Mayor is reported as saying that the school was in a very poor state when Dr White took over: 'Its condition could be compared only to the last flickering of an expiring flame.' In his farewell speech Dr White identified the need for 'more handsome premises' and he said that when they were provided 'there would be no place in the country that could show a more flourishing school than King's Lynn.' It would take another thirty-two years before the need for a new building was met.

The Lynn Grammar School in St James Street towards the end of the nineteenth century

The school was very much less successful under Dr White's successor, the Revd. J B Slight. Dr White had kept a very detailed account of the curriculum for each year group, term by term, from 1859 to 1874. This book shows entries in what I believe to be Mr Slight's hand but for only one year. Perhaps there were other records kept that have not been preserved. Or perhaps this is indicative of a less professional approach than had been the case previously. Certainly Mr Slight must have had much less business sense than his predecessor and by the time he left there were only 22 pupils on roll. In fact he left under a cloud. In 1887 he got into financial difficulties and was declared bankrupt. As a result the governors decided at a special meeting on 20 April that he should be given six-month's notice and dismissed. In the event, he offered to resign and this was accepted. However, there were problems right up to the end of the summer term. In May, for example, it was reported that the furniture in the school which belonged to the Head Master, was to be sold and, in early June, the governors were sent a bill for £11.14s, the cost of board and lodging for the Assistant Masters at the Temperance Hotel. It was decided that if this bill was not paid by the Head Master then the amount would be deducted from what he was owed in salary. Later in the month Mr Slight applied to the governors for an allowance of £4 per week, backdated to 25 May, to carry on the school to the end of term. He was offered £3 per week for one month to act as 'temporary managing Master' but this was to be deducted from the salary owed to him. Not surprisingly the governors decided that they could not agree to his request for a testimonial on his leaving the school in July.

As a result of the scandal and the low numbers in the school, the award of the Gold Medal was discontinued for two years. Its fortunes were however to be restored by the Revd. Walter Boyce and it was in his time as Head Master that King Edward Vll School came into being. His achievements are the subject of the next chapter.

2. From St James Street to Gaywood Road

The school as we know it really came into being under the Revd. Walter Boyce, Head Master from 1887 to 1919. At the Old Lennensians' Dinner in December 1928 he told members that the old school was falling to pieces when he arrived in 1887 and on a similar occasion in 1931 he said that it was 'a somewhat gloomy building utterly unfit for the boys to be there.' When he retired the situation had been transformed. The numbers on roll had grown tenfold from 22 to 250, the school's name had been changed and it had moved to a splendid and imposing new building. By 1906 when Mr Boyce presided over the move from the old Grammar School in St. James Street to the present building the roll had already gone up to 136 pupils.

The status of the school had changed in 1884 with the introduction of a new Scheme of Governance under the Endowed Schools Act of 1869. It was to be administered by a Governing Body of twelve: the Mayor of King's Lynn was to be an ex-officio governor; there were to be seven representative governors, appointed by the Prince of Wales, King's Lynn Town Council (2), the Trustees of the Municipal Charities of King's Lynn and the three Cambridge Colleges (Trinity, St John's and Emmanuel) linked to the school by endowments; and in addition there were to be four co-optative governors.

Walter Boyce was the first Head Master to be appointed by the new governors and not by the Mayor and Burgesses. As result he had to write to the Corporation to request the same privileges as his predecessor with regard to the occupation of the garden, opposite the school house. This was agreed in September 1887 at a rent of £4 per year, on condition that the exit from the theatre, next door into the garden was not blocked. He was also to have the key to the Greyfriars' Tower.

Compared with more recent times the involvement of the Head Master in governors' meetings was much less. In the nineteenth century Mr Boyce presented a formal report once a year in March and it was very brief. An example from 1895 illustrates the point:

'Gentlemen.

I herewith beg to present my Annual Report of the King's Lynn Grammar School.

I am happy to say that there is a considerable increase in the number. This term there are 72 names on the Books – 45 dayboys and 27 boarders.

Our list of successes for last year I think will most favourably compare with that of any provincial Grammar School of the same size. In addition to Cambridge Local and other successes, we had no less than six distinctions at the Universities of Cambridge and London.

While I can quite recognise the fact that a great deal can and ought to be done I believe that good sound telling work is being done in the School.

The health of the School has been uniformly good.

It only remains for me to record once more my gratitude to my colleagues for their able and loyal assistance.

I have the honour to remain

Your obedient Servant,

Walter Boyce, Clerk in Holy Orders,

Head Master of the King's Lynn Grammar School.'

Nevertheless, in the 1890s he worked hard to increase numbers at the school and several times persuaded the governors to extend the premises. For example in 1891 they agreed to accept a grant of £65 from the Norfolk County Council Technical Education Committee to fit out a laboratory. Initially it was proposed that a part of the schoolroom would be partitioned off but it was later decided that it would be better to put up a separate building in the playground and this was done early in 1892. The cost of this building was what seems a tiny sum today, £45 4s 8d. At the March 1895 governors' meeting, the Head Master submitted a plan for a building to be erected in the playground in front of the schoolroom because the teaching accommodation was insufficient for the numbers, which had risen to 72. At the June meeting it was agreed to submit an application for a grant to Norfolk County Council and plans for the new building were approved. In October the new classrooms were nearly completed and £150 was to be paid to the builder on account, the rest on completion. The payment of the balance of £45 15s was approved in March 1896.

A year later, in March of 1897, numbers were reported to have gone up to 93 and the Revd. Boyce asked the governors to consider the erection of a gymnasium. The cost of a corrugated iron building, 10 feet high and 50 feet long by 30 feet wide, was estimated at £220 and, at a meeting in July, it was agreed to go ahead if £100 could be raised by subscriptions. £54 had already been subscribed and Mr William Lancaster had promised to pay for the fittings. The project went ahead and less than a year later the Head Master told the governors that the gymnasium had 'proved to be a great boon to the school, especially on half holidays.'

His efforts to increase the roll were not however as favourably received as one might have expected. What seemed like a reasonable request in 1896 for an increase in salary on the grounds of the rising roll was referred to a sub-committee of the governors. In its report in October it proposed an increase in the allowance for Assistant Masters but no change in the Head Master's salary, 'taking into consideration the fact that Mr Boyce himself is the cause of the increase in numbers in the School.' What an extraordinary statement! In fact the system of payment was very different from today. In 1896 the Head Master received a salary of £60, free accommodation, an allowance for the Assistant Masters' board and capitation fees for each of the dayboys and boarders. Out of this he had to pay the salaries, the cost of board and other expenses.

R O Chapman (1904-06) in an article entitled 'Twenty-Three Years Ago' in *The Lennensian* (Summer 1927), described the schoolroom at the St James Street site as a depressing place:

> 'From the windows nothing could be seen but other dingy brick buildings in the surrounding back streets, while the scheme of interior decoration (if such drabness could be called decoration) could hardly be described as bright. This place was our sitting room, parlour, common room, or whatever you choose to call it, and after school hours there was nowhere else to go except the very prison-like schoolyard. Most extraordinary of anything were the desks….These venerable things, cumbersome and weighty, were a dozen or fifteen feet in length with very narrow seats attached; positively black with age and possessing lids (under which books were stowed) constantly in a state of disrepair. Almost every square inch of their surface had been cut with initials and names of generations of boys.'

He also describes the amalgamation, in 1903, of the King's Lynn Technical School, in Hospital Walk, with the Grammar School which meant that much additional classroom space and up-to-date equipment became available:

> 'The old building was then given over mainly to the classics, the Technical School being used for science; we had to walk backwards and forwards between the two schools for our various subjects. The playing fields were situated off the Lynn Walks and our school was thus located in three different parts of the town.'

Chapman's description was corroborated by Sir William Lancaster in a speech at the Mayor's Lunch, which followed the official opening of the school in 1906. He told fellow guests that the old school 'was in an entirely unsatisfactory physical condition. It was like the Irishman's coat – hardly a piece of the original garment was left.' It had 'a miserable little playground, not even tar-paved as they insist on in the elementary schools in London' and the sanitary arrangements 'were not materially altered' since he was there. Had it 'been an elementary school in London it would have been shut up years ago.'

Problems with the school accommodation were a constant source of worry for the governors. In 1900, for example, they discussed dry rot in the laboratory and in one of the classrooms as well as the poor sanitary arrangements. However, by March 1902 there was light on the horizon. The Head Master told the governors that 'the school buildings are in anything but a satisfactory sound state and we are looking eagerly forward to the time when we shall have new buildings.' At the same meeting the governors considered the copy of a letter from Mr William Lancaster to the Mayor in which he offered to 'build and present to the Town a new Grammar School' if the Corporation would grant a suitable site and agree to amalgamate the two existing schools, the Grammar School and the Technical School, opened in 1894, under one management. He felt that the town was not sufficiently large to support two schools. Needless to say the Governors were wholehearted in their 'high appreciation of Mr Lancaster's noble offer.' In 1903 the two schools were amalgamated under the name King Edward Vll Grammar School and a new scheme of organisation was issued by the Board of Education.

William Lancaster had been a pupil at the old school in St James Street in the 1850s. He had left at 17 in 1858 and joined the Prudential Insurance Company in London as a clerk. His salary was £15 for the first year, £20 for the second year and £25 for the third year. Through hard work and talent he became very successful. In 1874, at the age of 33, he became Cashier, Accountant and Assistant Secretary and by 1879 he was Secretary of the Company. In 1900 he was appointed a Director and he was the Deputy Chairman from 1910 to 1917. When he was invited to join the Governing Body of the Lynn Grammar School in 1900 he had already made several generous donations to the school, including the establishment in 1898 of a leaving scholarship, the Lancaster Exhibition, worth £30 per year, for pupils going to Oxford or Cambridge. A further donation in 1912 increased the value of this award to £50 per year. In 1906, the same year that he paid for the new building, he also endowed the King Edward's and Queen Alexandra's Leaving Exhibitions, which were worth £50 a year for four years at any 'Institution of university, professional or technical instruction approved by the governors.'

At a dinner to celebrate the centenary of the opening of the building in 2006 the guest of honour his great grandson referred to Sir William as a prime example of a Victorian success story:

> 'Sir William not only made a colossal amount of money, he followed the Victorian mould in his emphasis on education and the virtues of probity and hard work. In his extensive philanthropy he was also the product of his time and it is to the great good fortune of the people of King's Lynn that he decided to concentrate his generosity on the rebuilding of King Edward the Seventh Grammar school.'

The cost of the new building was estimated at the time to be between £50,000 and £60,000, although William Lancaster always refused to give the exact figure. It was a colossal sum in those days, especially when compared with the value of the old school in St James Street which was sold by auction in 1907 for £1210. In the newspapers at the time of the official opening in 1906 the building was described as 'palatial' and in a Board of Education Report in 1923 as 'magnificent'. It is an important building architecturally and today is a Grade II* Listed Building, protected by English Heritage.

The magnificent front elevation of the school, with the Boarding House on the left and the science block on the far right

The main K.E.S. building

The Head Master's house and the Boarding House

The proposed new buildings, an original drawing by Basil Champneys - it was clearly envisaged that it would face the main road

The building, begun in 1903 and completed in 1906, was designed by Basil Champneys, who is noted for his schools and colleges in the Dutch Queen Anne revival style. The entry in the second edition of *The Buildings of England – Norfolk 2: North West and South*, (Penguin,1999) by Nicholas Pevsner and Bill Wilson, describes the architecture in detail, including the Dutch leitmotifs, shaped gables, projecting side wings, round stair turrets and the ribbed barrel-vaulted hall. The section on the school also says that Champneys 'cunningly designed the façade to face the railway line to Sandringham, probably at the patron's suggestion.' This view is reinforced in a piece about the death of Queen Alexandra in *The Lennensian* (Spring 1926) when it is stated that the orientation of the school buildings was due to the express desire of their Majesties to obtain a full view of their architectural beauties on approaching the town. Certainly the original drawing by the architect shows the school facing the road. Despite Champney's reputation as an architect, Wilson is somewhat critical of the K.E.S. building, asserting that 'this school is neither as cleanly articulated as his later Bedford College, nor as charming as Newnham College, Cambridge.' The bronze statue of Edward Vll by W R Colton is described as 'baroque and slightly camp.'

The statue is a prominent feature at the front of the school, facing the main entrance. It shows the King seated on the throne and wearing his coronation robes and a hat known as the cap of maintenance. He is holding a sceptre in his right hand, upon which is a dove, symbolising peace. Edward was instrumental in bringing about the *Entente Cordiale* between Britain and France in 1904 and his role as 'Edward the Peacemaker' is also suggested in the design of the throne, on top of which, supporting a crown above the King's head, are the figures of two cherubs, one representing the home country and the other India. According to the description in the Listed Buildings Schedule, the cherubs 'hesitate because he is already wearing a hat.'

The original gateway is also of historical significance. The wrought-iron gates bear the monogram 'ER' for Edward Rex as well as the words 'King Edward Vll Grammar School.' Stone lions mounted on the brick pillars bear shields with two different coats of arms: that nearest the town carries the arms of King's Lynn and that nearest Gaywood, and therefore Sandringham, the arms of the King.

Because of the link going back to the 1860s, and, since the King had already approved the renaming of the school in his honour, it is not surprising that he agreed to open officially the new building. Unlike today when it is usual for one, or at the most two, members of the Royal Family to visit a school, hospital or other institution, to perform an opening ceremony or to mark a particular anniversary, the King was accompanied by the Queen, their eldest daughter, Princess Victoria, and the Prince and Princess of Wales with their two sons, Edward and Albert, as well as a large number of courtiers. Although the Royal couple, as Prince and Princess of Wales, had made several official visits to Lynn this was their first since their accession to the throne. The presence of three generations of the Royal House was taken as a great compliment to the town. As it turned out the party included not only the reigning monarch but three future monarchs, George V, Edward Vlll and George Vl. Newspaper reports say that the Royal party received a very enthusiastic welcome from the people who had made their way from all parts of West Norfolk to line the route. From the school up to Gaywood and along the Wootton Road there were densely-packed crowds, residents hung flags outside their houses and the roads were decorated with bunting. Shops in the town were closed from 11am until 2pm.

There had been many worries about the weather, which had been cold and wet for the previous week, but it turned out to be much better than expected:

> 'Royal weather, however, comes when it is least anticipated, and after a dull, grey morning, which threatened to develop into as dismal a day as its predecessors, the sun broke through the clouds, and the ceremonies were performed under the favourable conditions of a perfect autumn day.' (*The Daily Telegraph*, 6 Nov 1906)

King Edward, Queen Alexandra and Princess Victoria, drove from Sandringham in an open landau drawn by four grey horses, ridden by postilions splendidly attired in blue and gold with white buckskin breeches, and in front of the carriage, rode outriders in coats of scarlet and gold. Two other carriages carried the Royal suite. The Prince and Princess of Wales and their sons travelled

The King, the Queen and Princess Victoria in an open landau on the Gaywood Road

separately by motorcar. The Royal party was met at Wootton Gap by an escort of the King's Own Royal Regiment of Norfolk Imperial Yeomanry which accompanied them for the last mile and a quarter.

> 'With the addition of the military the Royal progress became one of particular brilliance. In its gradual approach from the distance the nodding yellow plumes of the yeomanry, mingled with the scarlet and gold and patches of white of the outriders and postilions, shone forth in bright array as shafts of sunshine caught them and thrust them into bold relief.' (*Eastern Daily Press*, 6 Nov 1906).

At the main gate the escort halted and the Royal party drove to the door between lines of men belonging to the 3rd Volunteer Battalion of the Norfolk Regiment who formed a guard of honour. At the entrance to the school the Royal party was met by the Lord Lieutenant of Norfolk and local dignitaries. The Headmaster and the architect, Basil Champneys, were among those presented.

Several hundred people were present in the School Hall for the official opening ceremony. The seats provided for the King and other members of the Royal party had been brought from the Town Hall and that provided for His Majesty was the chair used regularly by the Mayor until 1974. It is still used today at the Mayor-making Ceremony each year. Following a number of speeches The King declared the building open and then surprised everyone there, according to *The Lynn Advertiser*, by calling forward Mr William Lancaster and saying 'Mr Lancaster, I wish to confer the honour of knighthood upon you for the great services you have rendered this town.' Mr Lancaster knelt and the King touched him lightly on each shoulder with a sword. Shortly afterwards the Headmaster introduced the Head Boy, B H Binks, to whom the King presented The Royal Gold Medal, saying how glad he was to make the presentation on such an important occasion rather than privately at Sandringham as was usually the case. The Royal party afterwards inspected the new buildings and before returning to Sandringham the Queen unveiled the statue of the King by W R Colton, later a member of the Royal Academy, who was presented.

The King raises his hat to the welcoming party outside the main door

The arrival of the Prince and Princess of Wales and their two sons, having travelled to the school by motor car

The King on the stage in the hall reading his speech

The King knighting William Lancaster

Along with the official programme, a souvenir napkin was produced for the official opening of the school, one copy of which is displayed today in the school hall. It has pictures of the King and Queen and details of the programme: the drive from Sandringham in open carriage; the names of the suite in attendance and of the reception committee; the addresses to and from the King; the tour of the school; and the unveiling of the King's Statue. Unfortunately the information on the napkin is incorrect in that it refers to the unveiling of a statue of the Queen by the King!

None of Edward's papers relating to the opening of the school, apart from his speech, survive but there is a delightful entry in the personal diary of the Prince of Wales (Later George V) about his visit to the school:

'Mon Nov. 5 1906.

At 12 May, I and the two boys motored to King's Lynn where Papa and Mama opened the new King Edward Vll Grammar School, which had been built and given to the town by Mr W Lancaster, an old pupil. Papa knighted him at the end. We went all over the buildings which were extremely nice and up to date. Mama unveiled a statue of Papa. Got home at 1.45'

Note: Queen Mary was known as May among the family.

I have described this visit in some detail because its significance at the time cannot be overstated. Not only was this a major occasion for King's Lynn, but also the King took the opportunity to make a speech about the purpose of education which had national significance as illustrated by the headlines and quotation from *The Standard* (6 Nov 1906):

'The King on Schools - Noble use of wealth - Ideals of Honour for Youth - Debt due to England

It would be almost impossible to estimate too highly the importance of the visit which the King paid to King's Lynn yesterday to open the new building of the King Edward Vll Grammar School. On the one hand there was the hallmark of Royal approval set upon the completion of a noble project....on the other there was the remarkable address by His Majesty on the subject of present day education.'

The King's speech is reproduced below:

'I thank you on behalf of The Queen and myself for your loyal and dutiful address. It is a great pleasure to us to open your new building.

You are aware of the deep interest which I have always taken in the public institutions of the county of Norfolk, and in all schools established for the purpose of imparting higher education. It is not easy to over-estimate the far reaching benefits of the tuition obtained in such an institution as this. The young men of King's Lynn and West Norfolk whom you send out into the world will, throughout their lives, bear traces of the influences which have guided them during their stay in the school. They are at the most impressionable period of their life, and the teachings of your masters will remain in their minds even when later experiences are forgotten. You, as governors of the school will, I feel sure, exercise the most solicitous care in the direction of the studies of your pupils that they may be able to face the stress of life with an intellectual equipment, such as will enable them to hold their own in the world and bear their part in its work and duties with efficiency and to the benefits of others. Nor will, I feel confident, the higher teaching of morality, truth and self respect be neglected. The traditions of your school, dating back for so many generations, will help to foster those ideals, ideals of honour and patriotism which render this country respected in all parts of the world. Wherever they go your pupils will remember not only what they owe to you but what they owe to England.

These buildings are a proof of the gratitude of one of your pupils for the advantages he received here, and of his mindfulness of the importance of providing for his fellow subjects an education of the highest class. I know of no nobler use of wealth than its expenditure for the benefit of those who follow us, and no greater pleasure than what I trust will fall to the lot of Mr Lancaster in witnessing some of the results of his splendid example of public spirit and munificence. I pray that the blessing of God may attend the future of your school.'

The royal family taking their leave following the visit to the school

Sir William Lancaster and a group of Old Lennensians around the newly unveiled statue of the King

The land on which the school was built in 1906 was originally leased by the King's Lynn Corporation from the Trustees of the Municipal Charities, who owned the Almshouses on the Gaywood Road. In 1904 a 999-year lease was granted on some 7.506 acres (7 acres, 2 rods and 10 poles to be precise) of land to the south of the Gaywood Road at an annual rent of £90. In 1905 a further area of 6.122 acres was leased from T E Bagge by the Mayor and Corporation for 21 years at a rent of £26 per year. In 1912 this piece of land was bought from R L Bagge by the governors for £1250. Since neither the Board of Education nor the County Council would help with this purchase, the money came partly from the sale of some consols (government securities) and partly from a gift of £250 from Sir William Lancaster, who wished to save the governors taking out a loan. Another piece of land measuring 4.122 acres further to the south was bought from Major Bagge in 1921 for £825. Again Sir William came to the rescue and made an interest-free loan of £300 towards the cost. He also made sure that what was unpaid on his death would be written off.

Later in the century the Trustees of the Municipal Charities offered leaseholders the opportunity to buy the freehold of land and Norfolk County Council took up the option, paying £1800 in 1965, which seems an incredibly small sum today, for the original land on which the school was built. In order to comply with regulations relating to voluntary-controlled schools in the 1946 Education Act, Norfolk County Council then transferred the 3.75 acres of land on which the buildings stood to the governors. The final section of the playing fields, a piece of land, measuring 1.44 acres, was bought by NCC from the Borough Council in 1966 for £500. This meant that the LEA owned the part of the playing field furthest away from the Gaywood Road as well as an area close to the road. The Foundation Trustees own most of the playing fields and the land on which the main building stands.

For a period of seven years, from 1903 to 1910, the school was administered by the King's Lynn Corporation, through its Higher Education Committee. However in 1910 a new Instrument of Governance came into effect, which gave representation to the County Council as well as the Town Council and there were Foundation Governors representing the King and three Cambridge Colleges, Trinity, St. John's and Emmanuel. In order to qualify for financial support from the local authorities new regulations for the payment of fees were introduced. In 1910 this meant, for example, that free places were to be offered to one quarter of the number of boys admitted during the previous year. For each scholar in the secondary school a parent was to pay £10 per year and for those in the preparatory department, £7.10s. There were additional sums payable for 'printed' books and mathematical instruments. Fees were payable in advance and a term's notice had to be given before a boy could be removed. Requests from parents for remission of fees were regularly turned down, for example in March 1915 when a boy had been removed 'after the German air raid.' Fees had of course also been payable before 1910 and a further example of a parent being refused fee remission, perhaps somewhat harshly, occurred in March 1898. The governors' minutes read as follows:

> 'Read a letter from Mr J W Page of Hunstanton stating that his son had been a pupil at the Grammar School but had contracted typhoid from the water and that he had not been at school since October 20th and would be unable to attend for the rest of the term and also stating that he had paid £5 Tuition Fees in advance he asked for the return of two thirds of that amount as his Son was only at school a month, and it was agreed that Mr Page be informed that the governors cannot see their way to accede to his request.'

The interior of the buildings in the early part of the century is illustrated by the photographs many of which were published as post cards. The earliest additions to the facilities at the new school on the Gaywood Road were the provision of a cricket pavilion in 1912 and an open-air swimming pool in 1913, both proposed by Mr Boyce, who throughout the period of his headship aimed to improve the amenities of the school. The pavilion, which cost £150, was opened in July and paid for partly from a donation of £50 from the Old Lennensians' Association and partly by a loan from the bank, which was finally paid off in 1918. Mr Boyce suggested that the swimming pool should be paid for out of profits from the Tuck Shop and this was agreed by the governors, on condition that the plans were prepared by a competent architect and also that the pool would be screened from view at the ends facing the Great Eastern Railway and Tennyson Avenue. Incredible as it may seem from today's perspective, the hole was excavated by the pupils, working in gangs on their half-day holidays between 6 February and 3 March 1913. A contractor was engaged to concrete the walls and the base. An article in *The Lennensian* reported, 'Some tons of soil have been excavated by our sons of toil.' The pool was opened for use on 11 July. Those who spent so much time and effort digging out all that soil may have regretted it later, as swimming lessons turned out to be an

The main hall looking north with the stage at the far end

The main hall looking south and showing the tiered seating in the balcony

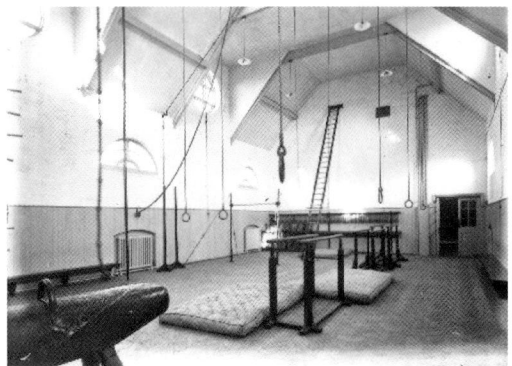

Views of the interior of the school; the art Room; the chemistry laboratory; the gymnasium; and a classroom

The interior of the Boarding House: the dining room; dormitories; and the boarders' day room

unpopular activity, according to various accounts by old pupils, although these are much later in the century.

The awarding of the 1906 Gold Medal by the King at the official opening of the school has already been mentioned. The school's Foundation Trustees are fortunate to have in their possession several Gold Medals, three of them from the first two decades of the twentieth century. One of them, the 1903 medal awarded to Frederick Dudding, is particularly interesting, since the original letter (dated 2nd December 1903) to the Revd. Walter Boyce from Sir Dighton Probyn, the Keeper of the Privy Purse, was kept for many decades in the school files but is now in the Borough Archives. This is the only letter from the time of Edward Vll which has survived, except one re-printed in *The Lennensian* (April 1908), congratulating the school on winning seven scholarships out of the fifteen won in Norfolk, more than any other school. The Royal Archive at Windsor has no copies of correspondence since Edward's papers were destroyed after his death.

Each time when a king has died the school has asked if the new sovereign would continue to award the Gold Medal and fortunately the request has always been granted. For example, in a letter dated 29th November 1910 to the Chairman of Governors, Sir William ffolkes, the King's Private Secretary says, 'that The King will be very glad to give an annual gold medal to the best scholar at King Edward Vll's School at King's Lynn, as his father did before him, and His Majesty will present the medal personally if he possibly can do so.'

A letter from the Keeper of the Privy Purse, 2 December 1903

During the First World War the awarding of the Gold Medal was disrupted. In March 1917 a letter from the Keeper of the Privy Purse to the Deputy Master of the Royal Mint said that 'owing to the present scarcity of gold', the King had decided not to present any more Gold Medals until the end of the War. This involved awards to some twelve different institutions including the Royal Society and the Royal Institute of British Architects. As a result of a special plea from the latter for a temporary substitute, it was decided that sand-blasted copper replicas would be produced. So the 1917 to 1920 K.E.S. gold medallists received copper medals and the gold replacements were sent to the school in 1923. It is not known if the medallists kept the replicas.

Another most interesting piece of correspondence from the Keeper of the Privy Purse concerned the Old Lennensians' Association formed in 1909. The first Old Boys' Dinner was held in December of that year and a report on the formation of the Old Lennensians' Association and the dinner is contained in the school magazine (March 1910) together with a copy of a wonderful letter to the Head Master:

'Sandringham,

28 December, 1909.

Dear Mr Boyce,

Much obliged for your letter of 23rd. I was glad to hear the dinner went off so well. I have since talked to Mr. ffolkes about it, and urged him, as I do you now, to endeavour to make this a 'standing festival'. I am sure it will be good for the school to have an Annual Dinner of this description regularly. I can always promise you, on the part of the King, a good supply of venison from Windsor Great Park for the Entertainment.

Yours very truly

Sir Dighton Probyn'

I am not sure how long the Old Lennensians' Association availed itself of this generous offer. When I told the story to then Keeper of the Privy Purse, Mr Alan Reed in 2005, he quipped that he was glad that the venison had been promised on behalf of the King not the Queen!

The First World War brought a range of problems for the school, not least the loss of teachers who joined the forces. Four had been given leave of absence by September 1915. Female teachers were taken on and there is a note in the records to the effect that 'the office' was to be set aside for the use of assistant mistresses and suitable chairs provided. Clearly they were not to mix with the male staff! The school buildings were requisitioned for billeting of troops during the summer holidays of 1915 and the playing fields were used for drill. But of course these matters were insignificant when set beside the numbers involved in the conflict itself, some 357, of whom 56 were killed. The War Memorial, paid for from subscriptions raised by the Old Lennensians' Association, was designed by an old boy of the school, Mr (later Sir) Guy Dawber. The mural, constructed in Hopton Wood stone (a light grey) with a centre panel of black Kilkenny marble on which the names of the fallen were cut and gilded, was unveiled by the Revd. Walter Boyce in July 1920, six months after he retired. It was reported in 1919 that Old Lennensians had been awarded 13 Military Crosses, 3 Military Medals, 3 Distinguished Service Orders, 1 Distinguished Service Cross and 1 Meritorious Service Medal, as well as 8 Mentions in Despatches. More recent research by Chris Dixon shows that 14 OLs were awarded the MC, 4 the MM, 4 the DSO, 11 were mentioned in Dispatches, and 2 were awarded the Legion d'Honneur, as well as the I DSC and 1 MSM.

In addition to the War Memorial it had been hoped that enough money could be raised to fund a leaving scholarship, but not enough was left when the bill for the memorial had been paid. Instead the £65 was invested to provide the *Pro Patria Prize*, still awarded annually. The intention was that it would be awarded, not so much for examination success, as for general character and contribution to school life.

The provision of a programme of out-of-lesson-time activities can be traced back to the early days of the twentieth century and the House system has always played a crucial role in this. It dates from September 1909, and was introduced as a result of a recommendation in an HMI Report following an inspection in June of that year. In fact the intention of the inspectors was that the school should create a pastoral care system, but it was also pointed out that the House divisions could be extended to games, which 'introduce a useful spirit of emulation.' At the beginning, the boys were allocated to Houses on the basis of where they lived. There was North House and South

The North House football team in about 1910

The victorious School House Football team in 1913-14

A school cricket team in about 1914-15

House for the Lynn pupils, Country House for those in Gaywood and the surrounding areas, and School House for boarders. In the case of the three Houses for the dayboys, even the House Masters were appointed because they lived in the particular residential areas. Inter-house sport was very important and from 1910 *The Lennensian* regularly carried House Notes with information about the matches and those taking part. The first Inter-house Challenge Shield, paid for out of profits from the tuck shop, was provided for the 1909/10 season and it is still in use today as the Football Shield.

The range of extra-curricular activities was limited by the size of the school and by the number of staff. Cricket and football were the main sports. In 1907, for example, there were cricket matches against King's School, Ely and King's School, Peterborough, as well as teams from North Runcton, Wisbech, Wolferton, Downham, Stow, Clenchwarton, Lynn Town, Hunstanton and Sandringham. Only rarely was the school team beaten that year, in one case by Wolferton, for whom the Head Master, Walter Boyce, took 6 wickets for 42 runs. First-eleven football matches took place once or twice a week in the autumn term and also in the spring term. A smaller number of second-team matches was also played. The latter had considerable success in 1907/08, only losing twice. They convincingly beat Wisbech Grammar School, 2-4 away and 13-1 at home. Sporting successes for individuals as well as teams can be traced back to the earliest days. In 1913 for example, George Gemmell (1903/07) was selected to play for England in an amateur international against Wales and scored one of England's three goals. He also played against France in Paris.

Non-sporting activities at this time were few. A Debating Society was started in 1908 and by 1910 a Nature Club was also well established. Music concerts and drama productions were regularly put on as part of Speech Day. However in 1913 when *Admiral Guinea* was performed it was reported to be the first time that a serious drama had been attempted. Another addition was music by the newly-formed school choir. In 1914 a Chess Club, a Boy Scout Troop and, not surprisingly perhaps, a Rifle Club were formed. During the War a school play was not performed every year but there were songs from the school choir, including patriotic music, such as the Marseillaise.

One of the major out-of-lesson opportunities for pupils was afforded from a very early period in the school's history by *The Lennensian*, the school magazine. Although it was edited by a member or members of staff, many of the contributions were written by the pupils and senior members of the school acted as assistant editors. It was first published in 1907, priced six (old) pence. The first editorial described its most important function as 'that of school crier and messenger, to call out and place on record the doings and un-doings of past and present scholars; in brief to act the part of *Gazette* to the little world, the microcosmic public, composed of all those directly or indirectly concerned in the affairs of the school.' It regularly included news about staff and pupil arrivals (*valete*) and departures (*salvete*), successes of various kinds, sporting fixtures and results, reports on events and articles, letters, poems and drawings from pupils past and present. I particularly like the cartoons which appeared periodically under the heading *As others see us*, for example in Number 2 (Lent 1908), *The Boy as the Master sees him* and *The Master as the Boy sees him*; and in Number 9 (Midsummer 1910), *The bowler as he appears to the batsman* and *The batsman as he appears to the bowler*. Over the years the magazine provided good opportunities for pupils to contribute as well as a wealth of information for its readers. Members of the Old Lennensians' Association automatically received copies of the magazine and this kept them in touch with what was happening in the school and with the activities of their contemporaries and other old boys.

How successful was the school under Walter Boyce? In the late nineteenth century the ability of the pupils was assessed each year by someone appointed as the official examiner and governors'

The Boy as the Master sees him' and 'The Master as the Boy sees him'

"We shall meet, but we shall miss him"

The Bowler as he appears to the Batsman' and 'The Batsman as he appears to the Bowler'

minutes included copies of these reports. In the twentieth century, Board of Education inspections became the norm and the first of these took place in 1905 before the opening of the new school. The report is very detailed and forms a basis for comparisons made in later ones. A brief report in 1907 said that the work was 'proceeding normally' but that the school had 'a difficult task before it to improve its internal organization and teaching up to the scale of its buildings.' It concluded that 'the successes of the school in public examinations, do not indicate that the teaching is as yet up to the level which it is hoped may be attained once the school has got properly started in its new existence.' The second full inspection in 1909 made a number of detailed suggestions for improvement and expressed the hope that the school would 'develop into one of the first grade, preparing boys direct for the professions or for the principal universities.'

According to the 1914 Report this hope 'has hardly been fulfilled yet...there is a tendency...to be content with a lower standard of achievement than what, with more determination, might easily be achieved.' This seems to have been due to the fact that boys were prepared for the Cambridge Senior Locals Examination in the sixth form and the Junior Locals in the fifth form, whereas the inspectors felt that the Senior Locals were more appropriate for the Upper 5th Form. However the governors were congratulated on the great progress that had been made since the last inspection, particularly the increase in numbers, the improvements to the premises and the excellence of the teaching staff. Some interesting statistics on the funding of the school were provided in the report, which showed that 46% of the income was from fees, 20% from the Board of Education, 31% from the Local Authority and 3% from other sources.

Despite the inspectors' criticisms, individual pupils from the Boyce era were successful in many walks of life. Students, albeit in small numbers, regularly won scholarships to the main universities and some became distinguished academics. The 1895 winner of the Gold Medal, Percy H Winfield, became a Fellow of St. John's College, was elected in 1928 to the newly created Chair in English Law at Cambridge and was knighted in 1949. George R Mines, the 1904 Gold Medallist, became a Fellow of Sydney Sussex College, Cambridge and in 1914 was appointed to a Chair in Physics at McGill University, Montreal. Tragically he died a year later 'in the cause of science', according to *The Lennensian*, March 1915. Frederick S Shears, 1909 Gold Medallist, who studied at London University and the Sorbonne, became a lecturer at King's College, London in 1921 and was appointed Professor of French at Aberdeen in 1926. Another linguist, Walter W Grave, whose name is still attached to the French Prize awarded today, won the Gold Medal in 1919 and went to Emmanuel College, Cambridge, where he later became a Fellow. He was to become the Registrary - the Chief Administrative Officer - of the University from 1943 until in 1952 he was appointed

Principal of the University College of the West Indies. Dr Grave returned to Cambridge in 1958 as the first Master of what is now Fitzwilliam College. He was also a good sportsman and Captain of both the 1st Xl Football and 1st Xl Cricket teams in 1919/20. Outside academia, Colonel G G Woodwark (1884-90) was elected as the Liberal Party Member of Parliament for King's Lynn in 1924 and he was Mayor of Lynn on more than one occasion. Another old boy at the school at the end of the nineteenth century had a distinguished career in the diplomatic service: *The Lennensian* (Spring 1938), recorded the appointment of Sir H A MacMichael (1892-97) as High Commissioner and Commander in Chief for Palestine and High Commissioner for Trans-Jordan.

The foreign languages teacher credited with nurturing the talents of both Shears and Grave, among many others, was Mr Arthur Thompson, who joined the school in 1906 and was there for twenty-

The 1919/20 1st Xl Football team, captained by W. W. Grave

six years, fifteen of them as Second Master (1917-32). He was one of only seven assistant masters when the new building was opened, although there were also four instructors - for Drill, Gymnastics, Writing and Geography and Manual subjects - as well as a Cricket Professional.

The Revd. Boyce was highly regarded by the students who passed through his hands during the 32 years of his Headship. This is well illustrated by his very generous leaving gifts. He was presented with a solid-silver tea service, a leather pocket wallet containing a cheque for £122 – a very large sum in those days - and a bound list of subscribers, some 400 staff and pupils, past and present, and parents. In 1922 the Old Lennensians' Association presented the school with a photograph to be hung in the Hall, although its present whereabouts is unknown, and he was regularly invited back to reunions of the Association. The fulsome tribute paid in the magazine when he died in 1936 also shows how highly he was regarded. It starts with a quote from Mr Boyce: 'And finally boys, remember always these three things – Always tell the truth. Never be ashamed to say your

The Revd. Walter Boyce, Headmaster from 1887 to 1919

prayers. Never run away from fast bowling.' A visit by Mr Boyce to Lynn for a reunion in 1928, eight years after he had left the town, is vividly recalled. As he walked through the town he was soon recognised and, 'ladies, tradesmen, old boys and acquaintances vied with each other to speak to him and shake his hand. Gone was their habitual stolid Norfolk reticence. They greeted him with cheery smile and ready speech. He was profoundly touched.' His love of cricket and his concern for the less academic pupils are highlighted in the article and perhaps the greatest tribute lies in the following words: 'Sir William Lancaster gave the school its magnificent outward body; it is not too much to say that Mr Boyce gave that body its soul.'

In 1936 a committee of the Old Lennensians' Association was set up to consider an appropriate memorial. The saga of the Boyce Memorial is a protracted and rather sad one. Nothing much happened for some time. A meeting was held in the autumn term 1937 and it was hoped that a sum of £250 could be raised to establish a Walter Boyce Prize. In the spring of 1938 it was reported that an appeal was being inaugurated. In the event, for whatever reason, it did not prove possible to raise the intended sum. Perhaps too much time had elapsed since Mr Boyce had been Head Master; perhaps the economic climate was not favourable. In the event, by the winter of 1939, the subscription stood at £41.14s. It was decided to try to get this up to £50 to provide an annual prize for success in cricket. However this was changed in the spring of 1941 when it was decided to purchase two seats, suitably inscribed, to be placed outside the boarders' entrance. Even this proposal was not carried out because of the lack of skilled craftsmen during and soon after the war. In 1951 the work was in the hands of a local firm but it was reported in *The Lennensian* that 'in these busy days their carpenters have to deal with the most urgent work first.' Finally at the end of 1952 an oak seat was presented to the school on behalf of the Old Lennensians' Association. It carried the inscription: *To the memory of Walter Boyce, Headmaster 1887-1919: A just and kindly scholar, who loved not least the friendly rivalry of cricket in these fields.* Even that was not the end of the story for within two years it was reported to be in need of repair. In the spring of 1955 it was removed to the pavilion while a concrete base was being made to receive the renovated seat. It eventually fell to pieces.

But the final word on Walter Boyce must not be a sad one. He had the great joy of seeing the school transformed. The early success of the school under the leadership of Mr Boyce ensured the award of the Gold Medal, which had been discontinued in the years 1887 and 1888. It was Mr Boyce who was responsible for the change of name in 1903 from the King's Lynn Grammar School to King Edward Vll Grammar School. At the Old Lennensians' Association Dinner in 1928 he told how, without consulting the governors, he had written to the King, because of the interest he had shown in the school, and that his suggestion had been favourably received. Three years later he moved the school to its present building in Gaywood Road. The school as we know it had been born.

3. The Inter-war Period

Mr C. L. J. Wagstaff

The Revd. Walter Boyce was succeeded in January 1920 by Mr C L J Wagstaff, who had previously been Head Master at Haberdashers' Aske's School at Hampstead. He was to be Head Master for the whole of the interwar period. There were 58 applications for the post and the governors interviewed six candidates. They were not unanimous in their choice but the influence of Dr Giles, the Master of Emmanuel, Wagstaff's old college at Cambridge, was probably decisive. It is quite possible that Dr Giles, a governor from 1914 to 1931, had persuaded Charles Wagstaff to apply for the post.

During Mr Wagstaff's time the number of pupils grew steadily. In 1922 the roll was over 300, by 1928 the school had 358 pupils, in 1930, 384 and, although numbers dipped slightly between 1930 and 1935, by 1936 there were over 400 on the roll. At the 1928 Speech Day the Head Master said that anything over 350 would make it impossible for the masters and pupils to know each other. In 1935, at the Old Lennensians' Annual Dinner, he indulged in a bit of name dropping, telling old boys that the school was getting too big and saying that he was 'inclined to take the view of His Majesty the King, which is that 300 should be the limit. With a membership of 300 a head master has a reasonable chance of knowing something about each boy; but when membership gets beyond that figure he can no longer do this.' The following term at Speech Day, Mr Wagstaff admitted that, although the number of pupils was at a record high, the number of post-16 students had declined considerably in the previous three years. He attributed this to the prosperity of the town and to the many employment openings available to boys.

Unlike his predecessors, Mr Wagstaff was not a clergyman. He was a physicist and the author of widely used textbooks, including one on *The Properties of Matter*. In 1922 he was appointed a revising examiner for the Joint Matriculation Board. Throughout his time at the school he encouraged the study of both science and mathematics. He was also responsible for the introduction of practical subjects and it was at his suggestion that the old fives courts were converted into well-equipped workshops in 1929, at a cost of £555 for the work and £383 for equipment. He said that the intention was not to provide vocational training but claimed that 'the nearest way to boys' brains is often through their hands.' Despite his views on the size of the school expressed above, it was this increase in the number on roll which made possible the introduction of the new practical courses. In his Speech Day Report in 1928 he acknowledged that in a small school the boys must fit the curriculum but in a large school it could be varied to fit the boys.

Many other changes to the buildings took place during his time at the school. In 1927 the rarely-used hall gallery with tiered seating – which can be seen today in a photograph hung in the Hall - was converted into a large and airy library at a cost of £572. The seats were taken out, the floor

The gymnasium after the fitting of the wall bars and beams in 1927

levelled and three sliding glass partitions fitted. The aim was to create extra space not only for the library but also a sixth-form teaching room. The old library became an ordinary classroom. Also in 1927, £100 was spent on equipment for the gymnasium which for the first time was fitted out with wall bars and beams.

Further changes were reported in 1935. The rooms formerly used as day rooms by the boarders on the ground floor of what is now C Block, had been converted into a Geography room and a classroom for the Preparatory Department, and the Lower Dormitory had become a day room. One of the two rooms at the top of what is now the Science Block was converted into a laboratory but the other remained an art room until it too was converted into a laboratory in 1972.

The 1658/59 stone from the time of Edward Bell

Towards the end of the inter-war period two stones, of considerable historical importance to the school, were built into the wall on either side of the main doors of the entrance lobby leading to the Hall. These stones, in the nineteenth century, had been located above the door of the school house in St James Street, surmounted by one showing the arms of Lynn. One of these stones was inscribed *Hen. Bell 1658-9 Linn Regis*; the other, *Rebuilt 1825 William Swatman Mayor*. As I explained in Chapter 1 Henry Bell was the Mayor when the first major rebuilding of the school house took

The 1825 stone recording major work on the School Master's house

place. As early as 19 July 1915 governors' minutes record that the Town Clerk had been directed to offer to the governors the stone taken from the Old Grammar School in St. James St. They decided that 'whilst accepting this offer, the governors should approach the Corporation with a view to having the earlier stone, now removed from the Shambles, also placed in the Hall of the school, thus securing the historical connection with former grammar schools.' Despite this reference to a stone from the Shambles on Saturday Market Place, which was pulled down in 1914, nothing more is recorded until 1938 when Mr Wagstaff mentions at Speech Day that two stones, although not the one showing the arms of Lynn, had recently been found and returned by the kindness of Mr S W Miles and Mr W A Bardell. The stones form a clear link with the King's Lynn Grammar School and it is pleasing that they were eventually incorporated into the present building. As early as 1926 in a letter to *The Lennensian* (Winter Term), Mr W R Bullmore, expressed regret that this had not already been done. He had been appointed to the Technical School in 1894 and, after the amalgamation, was a member of the Grammar School staff until he died in 1930.

The 1939/40 1st XI Football team. (This photograph clearly shows that the 1658/59 and 1825 stones have been installed on either side of the main door)

A major innovation introduced by Mr Wagstaff was what today we would call an 'open day'. The first of these Exhibitions and Conversazioni was held in 1923 in place of the conventional speech day. After the formal proceedings, which lasted no more than three quarters of an hour, Mr Wagstaff gave a short lecture on the gyroscope, after which parents and friends of the school were invited to see an exhibition of work, including pupils carrying out experiments. The stated aim, according to the Editor of *The Lennensian*, was 'to remove some of the preconceptions of schooling, derived perhaps from personal experiences of the bad old days, and assist in the creation of that co-operation and good will between the home and the school, so necessary to education.' Such open days, annual events today, were repeated at intervals in the 1920s and 30s. This seems very forward looking for 1923.

During Mr Wagstaff's headship several prizes were donated to the school, some of which are still awarded today. *The Pro Patria Prize*, mentioned in the previous chapter and funded from money left over when the bill for the First World War Memorial Tablet had been paid, was first awarded in 1922. Also in that year one of the school's old boys, Lieutenant Henry M Genochio (1906-14) was killed while serving in the Royal Engineers in Ireland and, in 1924, his father donated £50 to be invested so as to provide an annual prize in his son's memory. The prize was to take the form of either books or scientific instruments and it is appropriate that today the prize has become the *H M Genochio Prize for Physics*. In 1926 Sir William Lancaster made yet another monetary gift to the school when he invested £85 to provide annual prizes that could be awarded for success in games as well as schoolwork. Prizes for sporting achievement are today provided from other sources and Lancaster prizes are presented to students who are successful at 'A' level but have not been awarded specific subject prizes. Following Sir William's death in 1929, the Old Lennensian Association decided to fund an annual prize, to the value of two guineas, to be known as *The Lancaster Memorial Prize*. It was to be awarded, on the vote of every boy in the school, to 'the boy who in the opinion of his fellow pupils has most conscientiously played the game both in and out of school.' This democratic system of awarding the prize has long been lost but it is still awarded for significant service to the school.

In many cases the income from these early prize funds no longer covers the cost of the award and as a result the decision has been taken to withdraw the prize. This was the case with the *Firth History Essay Prize*, which was last awarded in 2000. Its origins are interesting however. In 1913 the Old Lennensians' Association collected £20 to fund a prize in memory of A R Firth (1892-95) who had died, aged 36, at Kobe in Japan. He had been a member of the diplomatic service and so the annual prize was to be awarded for the best essay on *British Interests in Asia*. Even in 1921 the governors realised that 'some modifications of the conditions regulating the award of this prize were highly desirable.'

Extra-curricular activities were an important feature of the school in the 1920s and 30s, and, as in other periods, the inter-house activities involved keenly fought competitions. In 1923 it was decided

School House in 1934

to introduce changes in the Houses, because the system of allocation no longer produced groups of roughly equal size and strength. This was because of the growth of the town towards the south and because increasing numbers of boys were coming from outside Lynn. It was decided to retain School House for boarders but to replace the existing North, South and Country Houses with three new ones: Thorseby, named after the school's first benefactor; Lancaster, after the school's second benefactor; and Keene, a distinguished old boy of the school, Sir Benjamin Keene, who had been British Ambassador to the Court of Spain in the eighteenth century.

A further re-organisation of the house system took place in 1934, because of the increase in the number on roll, which had gone up from just over 300 to nearly 400 in the eleven years since the last change. Two new houses, York and Windsor, reflecting the school's links with the Royal family, were introduced and all the boys, except those in School House, were re-distributed. Each of the houses was about 65 strong. Another factor in the change was the belief that smaller houses would give more opportunities to their members to take part in the various competitions. Each of the houses had a Latin motto, for example, *Per ardua ad astra* (Through hard work to the stars) was the motto of School House. It is of course also the motto of the RAF. It was surprising that Gloucester was not chosen as one of the new names at this stage since, as will be described below, the Duke of Gloucester had visited the school in 1931 to present the prizes and unveil the Lancaster Memorial Tablet. However when the number of houses was increased to eight in 1953, with the introduction of three-forms of entry, the names Gloucester and Edinburgh were adopted.

In the 1920s and 30s cricket and athletics - in the summer - and soccer and, to a lesser extent, hockey - in the winter - were the main extra-curricular activities on offer to the pupils at K.E.S. The inter-house competitions and the school teams' matches were written up in detail in *The Lennensian* and at the end of each season comments on the members of the teams would be published. In the autumn of 1926, for example, George Way (1921-29), the future Gold Medallist and Cambridge Soccer Blue, was described as 'a hitter who got runs on occasions. Safe field, but only moderate behind the stumps.' Cricket was clearly very much his second sport. The following spring, Arthur Wilde (1922-27), who played at inside half, received the following comment: 'Takes up a good position. Relies a great deal on his speed and consequently is not at his best on wet pitches such as we have had this season.' One of the best sportsmen of the 1920s was future Second Master, C M Bayfield, who went up to Cambridge in 1926, having been School Captain, Captain of School House and Captain of the 1st Xl Football, Hockey and Cricket teams. As one might expect, he also performed well in athletics. The commentary on Bayfield as a member of the 1st Xl Football Team in *The Lennensian* (Spring 1926) reads as follows: 'Splendid physique. Good leader. Powerful shot. Backbone of the Xl.' In later years he often played for the Old Lennensians' Cricket team when he was on leave from his Colonial Service postings.

From 1932 onwards there was an annual gymnastics display organised by Mr Freestone, the PE Master. The EDP report (reproduced in *The Lennensian*, Summer 1932) said:

'agile, white clad boys, with muscles of elastic and energy brimming over, treated an audience at the King Edward Vll Grammar School, Lynn, to an entertaining hour-and-a-half....The audience saw them go through a series of Swedish drills and then perform, with praiseworthy precision, difficult localised exercises, calculated to develop every group of muscles in the body. They climbed ropes, performed on ladders and treated the onlookers to some exhilarating, high-speed work over the beams and the vaulting.'

The 1st Xl Football team, 1924/25, captained by C M Bayfield

The original aim of the displays, held on three evenings at the end of the Easter Term, was to raise money for inter-school competitions. It was also proposed to award, in future years, gym colours which would have the same standing as those for cricket and soccer. In 1933, as well as general displays, 31 boys also competed for the Dennick Cup, donated by Mr J H Dennick. The first winner was A L Tabbutt (1931-34) and the eleven semi-finalists were awarded colours. In later years displays were also to be held out of doors.

An outstanding sportsmen at the end of the interwar period was Rufus Leggett who left in 1939. He had been Captain of both the school hockey and cricket teams and Mr George Martin paid fulsome tribute to his ability as a cricketer in The Lennensian (Summer 1939):

> 'A most accomplished batsman. His footwork, wristwork and timing are all admirable. His cutting is a joy to watch; his driving is extremely powerful. A good fast-medium bowler who has proved too good for most opponents. Should now learn to work the ball more. Admirable fielder. Whilst the claiming of records is always a hazardous job, I have no hesitation in saying that Leggett is the best all-round cricketer the school has yet produced. I remember Beaman, the holder of the school record of 211 not out against Ely King's School, Gemmell who made 181 against Marshland Rovers, Durrant, the Keyworth brothers, Barnes, the demon bowler, Shipp, Grave, Cross, Bayfield, Lenton, Langley, Barnett, and many other heroes of the past; but Leggett surpasses them all.'

During that term Leggett had scored a total of 639 runs in ten innings and had taken 49 wickets for

Gymnastic displays were an annual event from 1932

264 runs, an average of 5.4 runs per wicket. Rufus was to train as a teacher and for many years was on the staff of Gaywood Park School.

Hockey had been started up in 1921 and gradually developed as the second winter sport. It will be of interest to many present-day members of the Club that the first game proper was against a team called *The Pelicans*. Staff as well as boys often played in the hockey matches, since they were usually against non-school sides.

Other extra-curricular activities came and went. Some lapsed through lack of interest, others because they had been dependent on a particular member of staff who had left. The Debating Society was one which waxed and waned. There are references to it being revived several times after lapses of a year or more. One of the early debates, in 1923, was on the Channel Tunnel. The motion 'That it is the opinion of this House that the Channel Tunnel would be beneficial to this

The 1933-34 Hockey Team

The 1936/37 School Hockey team, including Mr Parry, Mr Hatton and Mr Miller

The 1939 1st Xl Cricket team, captained by Rufus Leggett

country,' was passed by 30 votes to 13. It was however to be another seventy years before the tunnel became a reality. The debates tended to be held in the winter terms as did the Film Shows and the other clubs, some of which were short lived. The latter included an Astronomical Society, a Radio Society, a Boxing Club, a Geological Society and a Historical Society. Chess was popular for several years but, like many of the other clubs and societies, it was for the most part boarders who took part. In 1924, for example, the membership of the Chess Club stood at 30 but only one was a dayboy. The same was true of the Rifle Club, first formed early in the First World War and revived in 1926. It became a regular activity in the summer terms but in 1930 of the 42 members only 6 were dayboys. This was partly due to the fact that the catchment area for the school was very large and many dayboys travelled to Lynn by bus or by train.

George Hern (1937/42) remembers having to leave home at 7.30 am in order to catch the 7.45 bus from Hunstanton and some of his friends, who had even further to come, cycled several miles to catch the bus. Returning home was sometimes a problem because by the time the bus reached the school from town it might be full and so the boys had to wait another hour for the next one. This would mean that instead of arriving home at 5.15 pm they got back at 6.15 pm, 'hungry, tired and with homework to be completed for the following day.' George confirms that living on the fringe of the school's catchment area had disadvantages as they had few opportunities to participate in the school's extra-curricular activities. 'I think that those living in the local area had a fuller and more interesting school life.'

In the Autumn Term of 1933, perhaps prompted by an HMI Inspection, discussed below, the Science Society was re-formed, with a regular programme of talks and visits. Over the next few years visits were organised, for example, to the Sugar Factory, the Gas Works, the Electric Light Works, the

Pumping Station, *The Lynn News and Advertiser*, the Co-operative Wholesale Society Model Dairy and Bakery, as well as to Bircham Aerodrome, the HMV factory at Hayes and the Pye factory in Cambridge.

Music for much of the period was somewhat neglected. For a few years just after the War a regular series of concerts was organised by Mr A M Gifford. As well as pupils, the performers included members of staff and their wives and daughters. One of the concerts, due to be held on 11 February 1922, had to be cancelled because of bad weather and was rescheduled for the following Saturday. Unfortunately it then clashed with 'the competitive fascinations of the Mart' which resulted in 'a very meagre attendance of dayboys'. However after Mr Gifford was dismissed at the end of the autumn term these concerts ceased and the only music for many years was provided on occasional evenings with gramophone records. At the very end of the period, in December 1937, a school concert was held but the band was hardly one we would recognise as such today. It consisted of a saxophonist, two violinists, a viola player, an accordionist, a pianist and a boy on drums. As well as various solos there was also a piece from a harmonica group.

It is not surprising that in February 1935, following the HMI Inspection in November 1933, which reported that Music was not part of the curriculum, the school received a letter from the Board of Education saying that there should be a 'musical life equal to that found in other schools of its kind.' A school choir, meeting regularly for practice, was, the letter said, essential. It goes on to suggest that a musical society, meeting twice per term, and an orchestra should be formed and that the upper forms ought to have an occasional period of musical appreciation. The appointment of a full-time music teacher should be considered.

S. J. Whitehead as Olivia in Twelfth Night, 1922

Drama on the other hand went from strength to strength and plays were regularly performed on two or three nights in December associated with Speech Day. 1922 saw the first in a series of Shakespearean productions, *Twelfth Night*, which was described as 'an undertaking far more ambitious than in previous years'. Sidney Whitehead (1919-24) made a very fetching Olivia (as shown in the photograph). Acting was clearly not just a passing interest for Whitehead, as the Spring 1927 edition of *The Lennensian*, in reporting his success in an examination of the Pharmaceutical Society, also mentioned that he was playing in *King John* with the Norwich Players at the Maddermarket Theatre.

There was no major school play in 1923 because the normal Speech Day pattern, as mentioned above, was replaced by an Open Day with demonstrations and exhibitions. However, in future years *Julius Caesar, A Comedy of Errors, The Tempest, Richard II* and *Henry IV Part I* were all successfully produced. One of the star

Macbeth, the 1933 school play

performers was Tom Valentine (1923-25), later a stalwart of the Old Lennensians' Association and for several years a school governor. As Brutus in *Julius Caesar* he was singled out as 'extremely good' in what was described as 'a brilliant success'. The following year he played Dromio of Syracuse in *The Comedy of Errors* in which part 'both enunciation and gesture were excellent.' The review continued: 'He captured the exact methods of the Shakespearean jester. It is no mean achievement to earn distinction in two such opposed roles as Brutus and Dromio'. The reviews were however not always without criticism. Of *Richard ll*, produced by Messrs Thompson and Cuthbertson in 1927, it was said that 'there was too much speaking of the parts and not enough interpretation of the meaning.'

By 1929 it was felt that Shakespeare should be given a rest and the production of a modern play, *Ambrose Applejohn's Adventure* was seen 'as a welcome departure'. It was a costly production though. The expenses came to £30.18s.6d, including a copyright licence fee of £13.1s.6d. However, the costs on this occasion were covered by the entry charge and a profit of £5.11s.1d was sent to the Lynn Hospital. This production was followed by *Lord Richard's Pantry* in 1931 - C E Cuthbertson's first solo production, although he had been involved since 1927 – and *The Green Goddess in 1932*. For various reasons, the chief of which was financial, the school had to revert to Shakespeare the following year with a production of *Macbeth*. I particularly like the comment in *The Lennensian* that 'rehearsing for the play had been retarded by the Inspectors coming at an awkward moment.'

Three short plays were put on in December 1934, including a musical play produced by Mr F J Bone, the organist at Sandringham Church, which was said to be the most popular. The drama productions not only provided good opportunities for boys who enjoyed acting but also afforded those with a more practical bias the chance to contribute, for example, to the production of sets and as stage hands. Eric Goldsby (1929-35) and Ronald Smith (1928-36) made some electrical equipment for the 1934 plays which would continue to be used in subsequent years. Sadly the 1936 production of G B Shaw's *The Devil's Disciple* made a loss of over £11 and the following year, and, perhaps as a result, a school concert replaced the play. In 1938 a school exhibition and conversazione took place on three days in December.

Another popular activity was scouting. There had been a scout troop at an earlier period but after a gap of five or six years it was re-formed in 1929 by Mr C A Freestone and Mr S R Beaumont, both of whom had joined the staff in September, and it was led by Mr Beaumont for much of the period after Mr Freestone became Assistant Commissioner for the area in 1932. As well as the regular weekly meetings the scouts also went on a summer camp each year. Southwold, North Wales, The Lake District, the Peak District and Happisburgh were among the venues.

Before the re-formation of the Scout Troop a general school camp had for several years been a popular feature of the summer holidays. Cowes was the base for three years and in 1926, for example, some 105 pupils were involved. Tours of the battleship *HMS Ramillies* and the liner *The Majestic* in Southampton Dock were among the attractions that particular year. Camps were also based at Keswick in the Lake District, Ilfracombe in North Devon and Heacham. I imagine a local camp seemed less exciting than the others. Mr Wagstaff often spent some time at the Summer Camp.

School trips of the kind that are very common today were rare in the inter-war period. However, for three successive years, in 1936, 1937 and 1938 parties of boys led by Mr Cuthbertson joined a cruise ship to Scandinavia. 25 took part in the first of these trips on the *TS Nevasa* and Trevor Jones (1931-37), who wrote a piece for *The Lennensian*, described the trip along the Hardanger Fjord in Norway as 'the most beautiful journey we could possibly wish for.' The trips were obviously very popular but the Second World War brought them to an end. Mr Cuthbertson was also responsible for the first of what became regular events in later years when he took a group to see *As You Like It* at the Maddermarket Theatre in Norwich in 1939. Again the war brought such trips to an end for the duration.

By the end of the decade extra-curricular clubs and societies were flourishing. There was the Science Society, the Debating Society, a Chess Club, a Musical Society, a Ramblers Club, a Model Aero Club, a Film Club, a Badminton Club and a Stamp Club. The last of these was given a boost in 1937 when H G Lemmon, the 1897 Gold Medallist, donated his collection of 10,000 stamps.

As the twenty-fifth anniversary of the opening of the school approached, it was decided that a list of headmasters from 1510 would be inscribed on a suitable board and hung in the school hall. This list was also reproduced in the special commemorative edition of *The Lennensian* published in 1931. Unfortunately there are several errors, particularly in the dates of appointment. The list seems to have been taken from H J Hillen's *History of King's Lynn*, (1907) and Hillen had not used primary source material. Instead, in this list, he perpetuated a number of errors made by earlier writers in interpreting the Corporation Hall Books. The errors are not surprising, since the earliest records often give dates in the form of a holy feast day and the year of a particular monarch's reign. Later Hall Books did use days and months but, until adjustments to the Gregorian calendar were adopted in Britain in 1752, the first day of a new year was Lady Day or 25 March not 1 January. Both systems of indicating dates in the Hall Books therefore have caused and still can cause problems for readers. Other problems were caused by difficulties in reading the writing and the use of different spellings of names and of abbreviations.

HEADMASTERS.	
1510. R. BURGH.	1750. C. SQUIRE.
1511. T. RIX.	1758. T. PEGGE.
1515. T. POKERING.	1746. J. DAVILLE.
1530. T. PERSON.	1755. J. KNOX.
1534. W. LEYTON.	1760. D. LLOYD.
1539. R. HALL.	1794. H. LLOYD.
1551. J. BACKSTER.	1797. R. SCOTT.
- R. JOHNSON.	1805. M. COULCHER.
1569. J. IVERYE.	1818. T. KIDD.
1590. A. ROBERTS.	1825. J. BRANSBY.
1592. N. ESTON.	1851. F. SCOTT.
1597. J. MAN.	1858. T. WHITE.
1608. H. ALSTON.	1874. J. SLIGHT.
1612. - ARMITAGE.	1887. W. BOYCE.
1618. R. ROBINSON.	1920. C.J.L.WAGSTAFF.
1626. A. FISH.	1939. J.G.LEATHEM.
1627. R. WOODMANSEA.	1945. S.H.GUDGIN.
1634. J. RAWLINSON.	1951. A.H.SLEIGH.
1637. E. BELL.	1976. R.D.GREAVES.
1678. J. HORN.	1990. M.J.WALKER

The board in the main hall, listing the school's 'Headmasters'

One of the main errors on the board in the Hall is the date of Thomas Person's appointment, which is listed as 1530 when it should be 1538, as should that for Sir Richard Hall, who preceded Person. The Hall Book entry recording the appointment of R Hall is dated the Friday before the Feast of Thomas the Martyr, 30 Henry 8th (that is the Friday before 7 July 1538) and T Person's appointment was confirmed at the meeting on the Friday after the Feast of Michael the Archangel, 30 Henry 8th (that is the Friday after 29 September 1538). There also seems to have been a mistake made in the spelling of the name of the man appointed in 1550, John Rackster, who is named on the board J Backster. On different pages of the Hall Book the name is variously spelt Racster, Rakster and Rackster, but I was assured by the Senior County Archivist that it is definitely an R not a B.

Perhaps the main error lies in the board's title – *Headmasters* – since for much of the school's history, up to the second half of the nineteenth century, there were only two teachers, the School Master and the Usher. The first use of the term in the Hall Books is in 1851 when the Revd. Francis Bagge Scott is referred to as the Head Master of the Grammar School. In 1858, following his death, the Corporation advertised for a Head Master to replace him.

The Duke of Gloucester's visit in 1931 to unveil the Lancaster Memorial Plaque

The centre piece of the Lancaster Memorial Plaque

One of Mr Wagstaff's most embarrassing moments must have been in 1930 when he gave the pupils a holiday to celebrate the twenty-fifth anniversary of the opening of the school. In December 1930 at the Speech Day he said that he had been 'under the impression that this was the twenty-fifth year of our existence; the boys willingly took a holiday for it, and it was not until afterwards we realised it was our twenty-fourth year.' The anniversary was celebrated the following year by a Royal visit. This was partly to commemorate the anniversary of the opening of the school by Edward Vll but perhaps more importantly to recognise the unique contribution of Sir William Lancaster to the school. Sir William had died on 28 February 1929 and a bronze memorial tablet had been designed and produced by the new Art Master, Mr H W Oake, who was also responsible for stained glass windows in All Saints' and St Nicholas's Churches. Speech Day had been postponed from the intended 5 November to Saturday 5 December so that the Duke of Gloucester, the principal guest, could attend. The Duke presented the prizes, unveiled the Lancaster Memorial Plaque and made a short speech. He was thanked by Mr Roy Lancaster, one of Sir William's sons.

During the inter-war period the Gold Medal continued to be the jewel in the school's crown. King George V had been present at the official opening of the school in 1906 and his personal diary records the presentation of the medals, which until the death of Queen Alexandra in 1925, took place at York Cottage on the Sandringham estate, since his mother lived in the 'big house.' One particular diary entry is of interest:

'Sunday Oct 16 (1927) Sandringham:

Gave my Gold Medal to Way's son the best boy at King Edward's School at Lynn, first time it has been won by anyone at Sandringham.'

George Way's father was a gamekeeper on the Royal Estate. George was one of only a hundred students in the country to gain a State Scholarship and he went to Emmanuel College, Cambridge to read Natural Sciences. As mentioned above, he also was one of the few Old Lennensians to gain a Blue, awarded in 1931/32 for Soccer. H M R Macmillan (1926-34) was awarded a Half Blue as a member of the Oxford Athletics team, running in the 440 yards and half-mile races against Cambridge in December 1936.

The 1933 winner of the Gold Medal was Eric Bales of Wiggenhall St Peter. When he took his Higher School Certificate he was awarded distinctions in both French and Spanish. The photograph shows Eric shaking hands with the Headmaster when the award of the Gold Medal was announced. At the time the press made great play of the fact that Eric Bales was the son of a farm foreman, having won a Norfolk Junior Scholarship to K.E.S. in 1926. Later in the year when King George V presented the medal at Sandringham he asked Eric if he played any sport and on being told that he played hockey is said to have remarked that he was probably too small to play rugby. According to *The Daily Express*, Eric told the King that he was '5 feet 1 inch in his boots.' The report goes on to say that His Majesty suggested to Eric that when he went up to Cambridge he would be in

Eric Bales (1926-34)

Eric Bales receiving the congratulations of the Head Master on winning the Gold Medal

demand as a cox. However nothing in his college record indicates any involvement in rowing. In 1934 Eric went up to Emmanuel College as an Exhibitioner to read Modern Languages. He won the Pattison Prize in 1935 and graduated in 1937. After a further year at Cambridge he sat and was successful in the Civil Service Examination, starting in the Inland Revenue in 1939. However the war soon interrupted his career and he was recruited to the Intelligence Corps. Tragically Eric died from meningitis in Weymouth Hospital in August 1942. His Gold Medal was returned to the school by his niece in 2012.

To the very end King George V maintained the tradition of presenting the medal in person. Although unwell, he still made the award to Eric F Thurston in the autumn of 1935 so as not to disappoint him. The king died in January 1936. Because of the upheaval in 1936, caused by the abdication of Edward Vlll, the Gold Medallist for that year (R N A Smith) was unfortunate in missing out on a royal presentation. Instead he received his medal from the Head Master at the Governors' Meeting in March 1937.

Over the years the Old Lennensians' Association has waxed and waned, as all these bodies do. They depend on a small number of active individuals to keep interest alive. The school magazine often carried appeals for information and ideas for new activities. In 1936, for example, it was a matter of concern that only thirty people had attended the Annual Meeting, although there were over three hundred members. Every year there was a problem getting subscriptions from some members and the amount collected in the previous year had only just covered the cost of the magazines and their distribution; the Annual Dance had been supported by a mere seventy old boys and their partners; and in the last six years the dinners had rarely attracted the numbers guaranteed to the caterers. However the cricket club was well supported and in the 1936 season the fixture list included twenty-nine 1st Xl matches and twenty for the 2nd Xl.

In 1938 it was proposed that the Old Lennensians' Association should establish a social club and so rooms were taken in the St James Street Club, offering facilities for billiards, table tennis, darts, dominoes, cards, chess, as well as newspapers and magazines and the opportunity to purchase refreshments. The subscription was 10 shillings per year for those within a twenty-five mile radius of King's Lynn and 5 shillings for country members. It soon had a membership of over sixty and a good level of attendance, especially during the winter months. However when war broke out in 1939 the decision was taken to close the club for the duration. It was re-opened in November 1946 but the membership was only half what it had been before the War. In the spring of 1947 it was decided that the club would only be open on three days per week to cut down on expenses and save fuel but this was not enough to save it. Later that year the decision was taken to wind it up and realise the assets. The world had moved on. One consequence appreciated by pupils at the school was that the billiard table was transferred to the Boarding House.

The 1939 Old Lennensian Rally was well attended, particularly as it included a farewell to Mr and Mrs Wagstaff, who provided tea for all those attending. They were presented with a silver coffee set and tray as a parting gift. The swimming pool, the tennis courts, indeed the whole premises were thrown open to members of the association but the main attractions, as in most years, were the cricket matches against the school 1st and 2nd Xls.

How successful was the school in the interwar period? Although the number on roll grew steadily, the numbers taking the School Certificate and particularly the Higher School Certificate did not change greatly over the period. In the summer of 1921 only three (out of five) candidates passed the Highers and sixteen (out of twenty one) the School Certificate. By 1937 the corresponding figures were four out of five and eighteen out of twenty five. The best Higher Certificate results were in 1933 and 1934 when ten students were successful from an entry of eleven and twelve respectively. Occasionally the Richard England Prize for the best Higher Level Science student in Norfolk was won by a K.E.S boy, for example in 1921, 1925, 1926, 1929 and then again in 1935 and 1936. 1935 saw the best School Certificate results when thirty out of forty pupils passed.

During Mr Wagstaff's headship there were two formal Board of Education inspections. The first, in 1923, was certainly not a glowing one. At a meeting with the governors in November 1923 the Chairman welcomed the Inspectors and expressed the hope that they would be able to give a good report. This hope was not realised! The Chief Inspector said that the school was not yet successful. There was no disguising the fact that hitherto the school had not succeeded in rising to the degree of success expected from its magnificent buildings and the degree of care given to it by the governors and the Local Education Authority. He said that the Head Master was an excellent scholar, a very good teacher and a charming man, but he had not dealt with staff in a sufficiently firm way. The staff was not a harmonious body, the masters were not pulling together and there were cases of men teaching the same subject who were not on speaking terms. These were nettles which needed grasping but the impression was that the Head Master had not shown sufficient strength in this respect. However they hoped that matters would come right as he was a good Head Master.

The second inspection, in 1933, was more favourable but certainly not uncritical. The general standard of work below the Sixth Form was described as mediocre. Science subjects were said to be stronger than the rest but French and Latin were weak. Some good work was being done but by fewer boys than were capable of it. 'The general level might be raised if the school took concerted action to secure the habits of industry and due progress during the earlier years of a boy's career.' However the assistant staff was not a strong one either in respect of their qualifications for the subjects they taught or of their powers as teachers. The inspectors commented that few of the teachers had had experience of other secondary schools and though they appeared 'willing to improve the quality of their work' they were 'handicapped by limited vision and lack of guidance.' They needed strengthening as a team by a few men with high qualifications and good organising ability. The Head Master was said to be a capable teacher with high academic qualifications, who knew his boys well and was devoted to their interests. He had done good service by maintaining the credit of the school during a period of constant expansion and by developing the work in his own subject area. However the school needed a 'stronger assertion of personal influence in the general direction of work and progress.'

On the positive side, the sixth form had 'been passing boys with praiseworthy consistency through the Second Examination and enabling those with suitable talent to go on to university.' The Inspectors also commented that the courteous manners, the appearance and the behaviour of the boys made a favourable impression. Despite the criticisms of some of the teaching and of the lack of progress in the main part of the school, particularly of the less able boys, the general conclusion was that 'judged by previous Reports' the school had 'undoubtedly made an advance in the last decade.'

Although the inspectors commented favourably on the behaviour of the boys it must not be thought that there were no problems of bullying or bad behaviour. There is a tendency today to complain about discipline in schools and it is obvious that some see the past through rose-tinted spectacles. There have always been children who would misbehave if given the opportunity. In the 1920s and 30s the threat of and occasional use of corporal punishment was a deterrent which ensured order in most classrooms but away from the gaze of staff and prefects it was a different situation. In 1934, for example, the governors received a report from the Head Master on the action taken against two boys 'guilty of unbecoming conduct on a motor omnibus when travelling from school' and a year later they received a complaint about 'the unruly conduct of boys proceeding home from school on public omnibuses.' Mr Wagstaff gave details of the steps he was taking to remove the cause of the complaint. One shocking example of systematic bullying from this period is described by Geoff Seaton (1933-36), who recalls new boys being 'taken into the cloakroom where a trapdoor was lifted to expose a tunnel through which the heating pipes ran – Down they went and the trapdoor replaced. One day a boy was dragged out unconscious – Thus the ritual was ended.'

Staffing seemed to have been a problem from early in Mr Wagstaff's period as Head Master. Immediately after the First World War salaries were not sufficiently high to attract enough good quality candidates to the teaching profession and many potential teachers had been lost in the conflict. In February 1920 the governors agreed that 'a lady might be appointed if no suitable man could be obtained' for a particular vacancy. This was despite the fact that at the same meeting they had received a complaint from a parent about the fact that his sons were being taught by lady teachers. However he also expressed general disapproval of the way the school was run and so the governors suggested that he should remove his sons elsewhere.

As the 1933 HMI Report had highlighted, many of the staff had been at the school for some time and had little experience of other schools. It was not unusual in those days for a man to spend his whole career in one school. This was true of G H Martin, who had been appointed in 1910 and retired in 1950, although he also fought in the First World War. Other long-serving teachers appointed in the 1920s and 1930s included T Gordon-Thomas (1914 to 1945), S H Gudgin (1920-51), C V Grant (1920-62), T J Bromhead (1921-55), F H Hatton (1922-59), W H Beaumont (1923-59), C E Cuthbertson (1927-54), L C Vernon (1927-69), S R Beaumont (1929-68) and C A Freestone (1929-54). These names will bring back many memories to old boys from several generations, some good, some less so.

One lady teacher, appointed in 1920 was Miss M E Place and she served the school well for over twenty years. Surgeon Rear Admiral Trevor Hampton (1941-48) remembers that she 'taught junior French very successfully, as well as securing unquestioned discipline, despite her quite un-spinsterish warmth and kindliness.' Professor Hassell Smith (1936-44) recalls an amusing situation concerning Miss Place, who took his class for singing, which he says she did with 'some verve.' Unfortunately for him she was also a friend of his mother, who had trained as a professional singer, and she would not accept therefore that Hassall could not sing in tune. He was regularly sent out to stand in the middle of the Hall for 'taking the Mickey.'

One teacher, not already mentioned, who seems to have been less than satisfactory was C G Gardner (1919-39). Jim Bridgment (1936-41), who was taught by 'Charlie' Gardner for mathematics in the first and second years, says that 'he did not actually do much teaching, just a few words to set us some work with a brief explanation…My first year Maths reports were simply 'Fair', 'Fairly Good' and 'Fair'. Perhaps he never marked anything. I think of him as a character straight out of Dickens.' Hassell Smith thinks that he was 'unhinged.' He says that he was 'known to everyone in the town, let alone the school, as *the green man*. He wore a green suit, his gown appeared green (probably with age) and he lived in a house which was painted green throughout….I think we all felt uneasy in his presence.' Robert Avis (1928-31) remembers him as 'a rather strange little man and an eccentric…he wore a short students' gown, a very odd garment, very threadbare and not very clean.' He was surprised that Mr Wagstaff allowed him to dress this way since 'he was so correct in his dress, as indeed were most of the staff.' His failings were obviously well known and Mr Wagstaff ensured that he was dismissed in 1939 before he handed the school over to his successor.

Another member of staff who proved to be a thorn in Mr Wagstaff's flesh over a protracted period was a Mr A M Gifford, a teacher of French, who, following a report on his teaching, was dismissed by the governors as from the end of the autumn term 1922. In 1923 and again in 1925 he sent letters to governors and various people in public positions criticising the Head Master. In 1923 he also wrote an article which appeared in the Lynn Advertiser making certain derogatory accusations, which were later withdrawn by the paper. A motion of full confidence in the Head Master was unanimously passed by the governors but they recommended that Mr Wagstaff take no legal action. As late as 1935 the governors were approached by a firm of solicitors in Carlisle asking for the case to be re-opened.

Mr Wagstaff is remembered as a very dignified man but, perhaps inevitably, one who seemed somewhat remote. Hassell Smith says that he was 'tall and imposing' and 'to a boy at least, he appeared formidable.' To Jim Bridgment he was 'the figure of ultimate authority.' Ron Linford (1925-30) reports that he 'had the engaging habit of walking absent-mindedly across the cricket pitch (glasses on top of his head as usual) quite oblivious of the match in progress.' When he retired, a tribute in *The Lynn Advertiser* (21 July 1939) referred to him as 'the great scholar and modest gentleman who, in a very real sense, has made the Lynn Grammar School what it is today

Mr C. L. J. Wagstaff, Head Master, 1920-39

– one of the great educational centres of England.' The writer acknowledged that public speaking was not one of Mr Wagstaff's strengths but 'one of his finest characteristics was that moral courage enabling him to take the strong line which he knew to be right though perhaps unpopular.' Although much of his time had inevitably been taken up with the administration of the school, he 'was primarily a teacher. He loved this work, and those qualified to express an opinion on the matter, considered him one of the best teachers in the country.' This is some accolade.

Mr Wagstaff lived to a ripe old age. In July 1951, at 76, he attended the school Sports Day. In October 1956, together with his wife and son, he was present at the 50th Anniversary Speech Day at which Osbert Lancaster, a grandson of Sir William, presented the prizes. He celebrated his one-hundredth birthday on 3rd March 1975 and was reported to be teaching himself to type. His death on 8 September 1981, at the age of 106, merited obituaries in national newspapers.

Charles Wagstaff led the school for the whole of the inter-war period. When he retired in 1939 K.E.S. was about to face many and varied problems, but it was to be a much younger Head Master who would face those challenges.

4. World War Two and the Aftermath

Mr J. G. Leathem, Head Master 1939 to 1945 (EDP)

Mr John G Leathem joined the school in the autumn term of 1939 from Marlborough College, where he had taught Classics to the sixth form and English and History in the middle school. He stayed for the five years covering the Second World War. Leathem was only thirty-three years old when he took up his appointment and he left in 1945 to become Head of Taunton School, where he remained until his retirement in 1966. There had been 165 applications for the post, a very much larger number than is the case today for vacant headships, and the expertise of Dr W W Grave, an old boy and Foundation Governor, representing Emmanuel College, was called upon to help with the short-listing. He first drew up a long list of twenty-three candidates of whom seven were recommended for special consideration by the appointment committee. Six men were selected for interview and Mr Leathem was the unanimous choice. He was to be paid a salary of £700 per year, rising by annual increments of £15 to £ 775, and to have the Head Master's house rates and rent free.

At this stage the school was still fee-paying, except for those awarded scholarships. A prospectus from the early 1940s gives the tuition fees as £12.12s per annum for boys under 10 years in the Preparatory Department and £10.10s per annum for older boys. Annual fees for out-of-county boys were £21. For boarders the fees, inclusive of tuition, were £73 for county boys and £82 for those from outside Norfolk. Fees had to be paid in advance each term. From September 1944 the fees for boys in Preparatory and Transition classes were raised to 21 guineas per year but, as a result of the 1944 Education Act, fees in the main school were abolished.

In September 1939 there was a proposal by the Local Education Authority to close the King's Lynn Girls' High School during the War and have the girls taught on the Grammar School premises. The Head Mistress, Miss Williamson, was very much against this idea and persuaded both sets of governors, at a joint meeting, to oppose it. The fact that this scheme did not go ahead made it possible for the transfer to K.E.S., on 18 October 1939, of the pupils of London's Hackney Downs School, originally billeted in Upwell and Outwell, where they had been expected to use the totally inadequate facilities offered by the village schools.

Some 320 boys from Hackney Downs Grammar School were evacuated to Lynn in 1939 and, although the numbers soon fell as parents took their sons back to London following the 'phoney war' of 1940, the school stayed in Lynn until 1945. Initially, the governors asked the Hackney Downs staff to find alternative playing fields because of the worn condition of the K.E.S. fields in winter but from 1941 they did use the school fields for sport at agreed times. The swimming pool however was not made available. Perhaps they should not have been too disappointed at this refusal. Anthony Avis (1938-45) in his *Reminiscence of King Edward Vll Grammar School*, (1991), describes shivering to death in ice-cold chlorinated water for half an hour and then being unable to dry himself and dress in time for the next lesson. He says that 'swimming was not a sport or activity which was greeted with much enthusiasm'. On the other hand the pool clearly provided a lot of enjoyment for some, as archive photographs show. Unfortunately it has not been possible to date them.

Summer fun in the swimming pool

Until the autumn term of 1943, when the Technical Institute in Lynn became available, the Hackney Downs boys had to be accommodated for lessons. Up to the end of 1940, by which time the numbers had fallen considerably, the K.E.S. boys were taught in the mornings and the Londoners in the afternoons, from 1.15 to 5 pm. Even after the main part of the London school was moved, the Science Sixth continued to use the K.E.S. laboratories, since an arrangement had been made in 1941 to share the teaching of Chemistry and Mathematics in the Sixth Form. Because so many boys had gone back to London it was decided to re-open the Hackney Downs site in 1943 and 135 boys were taught there by seven masters. It had been intended that the rest of the pupils and staff would return to London in 1944, but when the flying-bomb attacks started in London, many parents sent their sons back to Lynn so that numbers went up to 140 for the last year of the evacuation. Before leaving in 1945 the Head Master, Mr Balk, spoke of 'a very pleasant connection' with K.E.S. and paid a warm tribute to Mr Leathem and his staff for the way in which they had dealt with 'the difficult and harassing days of evacuation.'

The boys digging trenches on the school field in the autumn term of 1939

The possibility of air attacks or German invasion were accepted from the beginning of the War and during the autumn term preparations were made, including the digging of trenches in the grounds, the darkening of the windows in the boarding wing and the provision of a gas-proof room. A fire-watching rota of staff and boys (from both schools) was introduced in the spring of 1941 and the building was regularly patrolled during the night. The volunteers had to be aged 16 and the bonus was that they were paid three shillings per night. There was also a rota for the summer holidays. An article in *The Citizen* (5 August 1992) recalls these *Wartime duties for KES boys*.

'Many of the senior boys volunteered for fire-watching duties at the school. Each night one member of staff and four boys stayed overnight. The staff members used the headmaster's office for access to the telephone and for sleeping. It was one of only three rooms that was blacked out. No lights were permitted elsewhere as they might have been seen from the air. Two nearby classrooms were also blacked out for the use of the boys, one for sleeping in, two at a time, while the other two were alert. We had been trained to use stirrup pumps on fire bombs. For this purpose we had to know the way round the school and the roof in darkness….Many of us made a point of going on the roof each time we were on duty. Partly this was in order to ensure full familiarity in case of need, partly for the view and partly for the dare-devil thrill of walking round the top of the two corner towers in the dark. This was of course forbidden. Access to the roof was by metal rungs on an outside wall of the building. It was also possible to enter the roof space by this route.'

Disaster struck in 1942 when the school was hit by at least five incendiary bombs in the early hours of 30 June. The roofs of the north and south blocks and the main building were all hit. The roof of the main building, which suffered only slight damage, was saved by the courage and initiative of the school fire watchers. Two boys, Richard Warner (1936-45) and Gerald Sandover (1933-44) climbed out onto the roof to try to dislodge a fire bomb which was wedged under the tiles. Another boy, Freddie 'Pip' Silk (1934-43), helped from inside the roof. The boys on the roof were joined by the caretaker, Mr Greenacre, and two policemen with a stirrup pump. In letters to Mr Leathem the staff and boys were commended by the Divisional Fire Officer and Lynn's Chief Fire Watcher for their prompt action. The latter said that 'their courage and initiative undoubtedly saved the main hall and they made a valiant attempt to save the science block. It is largely due to their efforts that the fire was held back until other help arrived.'

The science laboratory, 30 June 1942 (Lynn News)

Firemen from Gaywood tackled the north block, which was on fire when they arrived. While they were attending to this section of the school, fire broke out in the roof of the Boarding House and this developed much more seriously. Unfortunately one of the local fire engines had an accident at the Gaywood clock on its way to the school and it was left to firemen from Wisbech, when they eventually arrived, to deal with the Boarding House. There was considerable damage to the north

The upper corridor of the Boarding House littered with debris (Lynn News)

The senior dormitory was completely gutted (Lynn News)

The roof of the Boarding House was destroyed (Lynn News)

block but part of the roof was saved, whereas that on the south block was completely burnt out. The firemen did however manage to stop the fire spreading to the Head Master's house. The fire and water, used to douse the flames, played havoc with the top floors of the buildings and with the contents of the lower ones. Thankfully there were no casualties.

One story about the fire-bombing, retold in *The History of Hackney Downs School* by Geoffrey Alderman, (The Clove Club, 1972,) concerns that school's biology master, Mr Gee, who taught in the junior science room at the top of the science block. The fire-bombing had occurred during the period of the School Certificate examinations and he 'decided that his specimens were in grave danger, as the jets from the water hoses were not powerful enough to break the windows of the room in which the specimens were kept. With calm deliberation he sought out a shotgun…and successfully shattered the glass. This timely action saved the specimens but resulted in a summons to appear before the magistrates on a charge of being in possession of a firearm and discharging it to the danger of the public.' Fortunately the case was dismissed with 'an official warning from the bench but with unofficial praise and congratulations.' This story is also told by Vic Allen (1934-42), the senior prefect on duty that night in June 1942. In *Lets Talk!* (August 2004), published by Archant Press, he also spills the beans, saying that the boarders who went out on to the roof and did such sterling work knew how to get up there from earlier 'illegal excursions for a quiet smoke.'

Before leaving the topic of Hackney Downs School I should perhaps put the record straight about the actor Michael Caine, who many people seem to think was a pupil at K.E.S. He was not.

Maurice Micklewhite, as he was then called, was evacuated to Lynn during the war and records show that he passed the London County Council scholarship examination when he was a pupil at North Runction School in 1944. He did however attend Hackney Downs School in Lynn during 1944/45.

As a direct result of the fire-bombing there was an immediate need for temporary accommodation for the boarders and they were moved to 123 Gaywood Road, which the military authorities agreed to give up for the remainder of the term. On 23 July 1942 HRH the Duke of Kent paid a visit to the school and to other parts of the town to see the damage caused by the fire-bombing. Only a few weeks later he was killed in a plane crash.

Emergency repairs to the damaged roofs were urgently needed but there were inevitable delays. In September 1942 the contractor was unable to obtain the licence for necessary materials, in particular timber, despite approval from the Board of Education to go ahead; by November the materials had arrived but there was a problem in recruiting labour 'for roof work on so lofty a building'. However by February 1943 Mr Leathem was able to report satisfactory progress with the repairs and they were finally completed during the following month. The cost of these temporary repairs, which came to over £1900, was met by the War Damage Commission, although the first part-payment did not arrive until September 1943 and the balance of the money not until July 1944. The Commission also refused to pay £73.7s.11d for work which they did not consider to be temporary.

During the War period the roll fluctuated but there was an overall increase from 375 in 1939 to 418 in 1945. The number of boarders was a cause for concern for several years, falling to as low as 18 in 1940 but, although this made the Boarding House uneconomic, the governors decided to keep it open. One reason for the low number at the beginning of the War was that foreign pupils who had been recruited in the past were no longer able to come to England. Fortunately by 1943 the number of boarders had gone back up to 45 and the question of closure disappeared.

Another consequence of the War, as in 1914-18, was that teaching vacancies had sometimes to be filled by women. It was reported in September 1940 that a room was to be set aside for the use of lady members of staff. One wonders where Miss M E Place had been sitting all those years! She had been a teacher at the school since 1920 and from 1927 to the summer of 1939 had been joint editor of *The Lennensian*. Miss Place retired in 1942.

A change which was not attributable to the War was the closure of the workshops at the end of the summer term, 1940. There had been a Board of Education inspection in March which had found both the teacher in charge, Mr S A Parry, and the tools and equipment unsatisfactory. At first the governors intended to suspend the teaching of metalwork and re-equip the woodwork room. However, having obtained information on the costs involved they decided to close both workshops and ask Mr Parry to resign. Later in the War the metalwork room became an overflow dining room.

In 1940 Norfolk County Council indicated its intention to provide mid-day meals in all its secondary schools and K.E.S. was asked to co-operate. By November meals were being provided on three days per week for over 100 boys and the dining room and kitchen were being used to full capacity. From 1943 the former metalwork room had to be used for lunches and by 1945 150 boys were being served every day. It took a long time before alternative accommodation was provided. In September 1944 the school had asked the Education Authority to expedite the delivery of the promised pre-fabricated canteen and kitchen; a year later it was reported that the erection was progressing. Yet it took until May 1946 before it was ready for use.

As in the First World War, the award of the Gold Medal was affected by scarcity of gold. The Gold Medal winners from 1940 to 1946 missed the personal presentation. Despite a letter to Mr Leathem, the Headmaster, in 1939, indicating that the award of the medal would continue during the war, a further letter in 1940 stated that it had been decided that, in the national interests, the issue of gold had to be restricted. No gold medals were struck by the Royal Mint during the rest of the War. The Gold Medal winners received certificates instead. From 1940 to 1944 these indicated that the medals would be presented after the War; those for 1945 and 1946 said that the medals would 'be forwarded when circumstances permit'. In the event, all the Gold Medals for 1940 to 1946 were sent by registered post in 1947. So the War had unfortunate ramifications for the Gold Medallists.

Not only was gold scarce but so also were all kinds of metal. By the end of 1940 the World War l German howitzer, a familiar feature at the front of the school in the 1920s and 30s, had been removed by the Ministry of Supply, presumably to be melted down. It had been on the site since 1919, in the 'safe care and custody' of the school, having been offered to the town by the War Office Trophies section.

Examination results during this period were far from spectacular and, as before the War, numbers in the sixth form were small. The best results in the Higher School Certificate were in 1942 when all five candidates were successful, with four of them doing well enough to be awarded Major County Scholarships. Despite small numbers individual K.E.S. pupils often did extremely well, for example in 1940 A G Searle (1935-40) won the Richard England Prize, awarded for the best science results in Norfolk. 1942 might have been a good year for the Highers but it was the poorest year for the School Certificate results with only 22 passes out of an entry of 43. Mr Leathem had reported to the governors in June that the B forms lacked keenness and when the results were published his concern was shown to be justified: only 3 boys out of 19 from Form VB had passed.

During the War extra-curricular activities were hit by a range of problems, not least the shortage of rooms during the period when Hackney Downs School shared the premises. The damage caused by the fire bombs dropped on the school in 1942 also caused disruption. Nevertheless, weather permitting, a relatively full programme of sport took place, both as part of the inter-house activities and with matches against teams from outside the school, including many RAF teams. In one sense the presence of Hackney Downs School was an advantage as they provided teams against which the K.E.S. boys could play on a regular basis. Mr Leathem was a keen sportsman, frequently on the field, either as the mainstay of the hockey side when playing adult teams such as the RAF or the police, or as a spectator at house or school matches. Other regular staff members of the hockey team included Mr Freddie Hatton and Mr Stanley Beaumont.

The House Masters were in the main the same ones as had been in post in the previous decade: Mr Cuthbertson (School House); Mr Freestone (Keene); Mr Gordon-Thomas (Lancaster); Mr Hatton (Thoresby); Mr Bromhead (Windsor); and Mr Vernon (York). These men played a vital role in the co-ordination and encouragement of the inter-house programme which has always been an important part of the extra-curricular activities offered to K.E.S. pupils. They were often responsible for developing many other opportunities for the benefit of the boys. Mr Hatton, for example, established the school Cadet Corps in 1942, with the help of Messrs Vernon and Cuthbertson. The latter was the Editor of *The Lennensian*, ran the school library and was producer of the school plays, as well as supporting some of the other clubs and societies. Mr Gordon-Thomas was the organiser of the Chess Club and helped many of the younger boys to learn how to play. 'Pop'

Freestone had started up the Scout Troop in the 1930s and continued to organise the annual gym display and competition for the Dennick Cup. During the War he was responsible for setting up the local area Air Cadet Corps and 1943 was made an M.B.E.

The Head Master and the teaching staff in 1945

The Army Cadet Corps became an important part of school life in the 1940s and 1950s and at its peak it had over a hundred members. In 1943 it was listed as *The Royal Norfolk Regiment, 2 Company, 3rd Cadet Battalion*. Weekly meetings were held at which the boys developed a range of skills as well as taking part in the inevitable drills. An annual camp was held for cadet units across the county but attendance from Lynn varied. In 1943 nearly 50 cadets went on the camp held at Attlebridge. However, the following year when the camp, which had some 750 participants,

The Army Cadet Force in 1942

was held at Fritton near Yarmouth, the number from K.E.S. was relatively small. A rather tongue-in-the-cheek report in *The Lennensian* put this down to the fact that farmers could not be persuaded to have their harvests at some other time of the year!

During the War members of the school did get involved in farming. In 1941 part of the playing field near to the railway line was ploughed up with the help of Mr R H Kerkham, a local farmer and school governor, and in subsequent years the cultivated area was extended. In 1943 the Head Master reported that a very good crop of vegetables was being produced and used in the school kitchen. Also in 1941, for the second year running, arrangements were made for volunteers to help with the harvest in the summer holidays. More than 70 boys made their own arrangements and a further 35 to 40 were placed by Mr Cuthbertson on farms as far as Sporle and Burnham Overy. They were boarded at the houses of the foremen or in other billets and Mr Cuthbertson, Mr Vernon or Mr Whitehead visited then each week to check that all was well. Complaints were few and the farmers spoke highly of the boys' work. Almost all stayed for five weeks although they had only volunteered for four. They were paid for the work and so both sides were well pleased. This involvement continued for the rest of the War.

Mr J. G. Leathem and the prefects in 1945

As mentioned above, Mr Cuthbertson had for many years produced an annual school play. During the War the drama productions were not as regular or as ambitious as they had been in the previous decade. In March 1941 three short plays were put on, including the musical, *The Charcoal Burner's Son*, produced by Mr Bone, which was said to have been a great success when it was first performed in 1934. This pattern of three short plays was repeated in December 1941 and again at the end of 1944.

Mr Leathem encouraged the musical life of the school. A series of concerts, organised by Mr Grant, was held in 1940 and 1941 but then music was somewhat neglected until 1944 when Mr Bone formed a Musical Society. A Rhythm Club was started in 1941 to play records and to listen to boys playing jazz; it soon lapsed but it too was re-formed in 1944. Clubs and societies which had been in existence in the 1930s, such as the Science Society, the Chess Club, the Stamp Club and the Debating Society, continued during the War, although with varying degrees of success and all had periods when they were inactive. In the summer terms the Tennis Club was popular but sometimes the opening of the courts was delayed by the difficulty of obtaining equipment. One formerly popular group, the Scout Troop, which had been active for ten years, was not revived after being suspended in the autumn of 1939. A clear casualty of the War was the Ramblers Club formed in 1938. Particularly after the second half of the summer term 1940, when signposts were removed in case of an invasion, rambling and cycling were practically impossible.

In 1945 Mr Gordon-Thomas retired after 30 years at the school. As well as being in charge of Lancaster House for twenty-two years, he had organised weekly film shows, encouraged chess players, stage managed plays, run the rifle club and during the War had taken on responsibility for the air-raid precautions and the organisation of fire-watching. He had also been a teacher who inspired affection and respect as illustrated by the Editor in *The Lennensian* in July 1945: 'Not an Old Boy visits the school but asks where to find G.T., not an Old Boy writes from Germany, from India, from the Middle East but asks 'How is G.T.?' He was not so favourably remembered by Professor Hassell Smith (1936-44) who recalls him rushing about the school, gown billowing behind him, often arriving twenty minutes late for the geography lesson he was supposed to be teaching. He would set some work and then either busy himself at his desk or vanish again. Smith says his cousin, Norman Eagleton (1921-29), who was a distinguished pilot in Coastal Command during the War, summed Gordon-Thomas up well with the words, 'He's the busiest man I've ever known but I'm damned if I know what he does.' Jim Bridgment (1936-41) also remembers GT spending a lot of time out of the classroom. The class was often set work and then left to get on with it. He remembers listening to BBC schools' broadcasts, including ones in 1938/39 about the economic progress being made in Germany. Looking back on it he finds it bizarre that they listened to programmes such as *The People's Car* when 'there was a war going on in Spain which provided practice for the Luftwaffe.' GT's place as the Lancaster House Master was taken by Mr W H Beaumont, who had returned to the school in the spring after serving in the army since 1939.

Mr Leathem was the only Head Master in the twentieth century who left to take up a post in another school; all the others retired. It was not an easy period for very obvious reasons. In a tribute to his work in *The Lennensian* (July 1945) the six years of his headship are described as 'among the most difficult the school can have ever known. Two schools using one building, air-raid precautions, shortages of all kinds, frequent changes of staff, fire and damage by night, these are but a few of the things with which Mr Leatham has had to cope.'

Views on Head Masters are rarely unanimous. Michael Kisby, who left for City of Norwich School at the end of the 3rd year in 1941, does not recall Mr Leathem as kindly as some: 'I still remember Mr Leathem in a Latin class in 3A described me as a little duffer in front of the class.' On the other hand, Ivan Levey (1936-44) recalls Leatham as 'a most considerate and helpful headmaster' who made it possible for him to get on an Air Ministry course at university, despite having missed his final school examinations, because he had already joined the RAF. Tony Avis, who was also at the school during the war years, says that he got a place at Cambridge largely as a result of the influence of Mr Leathem: 'I was considered the most unlikely of our limited sixth form to get a university place….I shall be ever grateful to him for bringing about the most significant event in my life.' An amusing tale is told by John Frost (1939-44) following complaints from a number of boys about the swimming pool being cold: 'Mr Leathem – bless him – listened – walked us to the pool – changed – did one length – ahh –changed our TT from 1st period Mon am when the pool was still being filled from the mains. Later he walloped us! (saying) 'Do first, argue next". I related in the last chapter how Hassell Smith had regularly been made to stand in the hall by Miss Place because, knowing his mother had an excellent voice, she thought he sang out of tune deliberately. He says that it was to Leathem's credit that, after interrogating him two or three times, 'he saw the funny side of it and together we would have a chuckle.'

Following the resignation of Mr Leathem, Mr E A G Marlar, Head of King Edward Vl School in Litchfield, was appointed to take up the post from January 1946. In the interim the Second Master, Mr S H Gudgin, was to be Acting Head. As it turned out, Mr Marlar never took up the appointment. He had been offered an allowance of £150 to take overall responsibility for the Boarding House, £50 of which would cover the use of the Head Master's house, rent (but not rate) free. The House Master, Mr Cuthbertson was to receive £50 plus free board and lodging for the day-to-day supervision of the boarders. At quite a late stage Mr Marlar wrote to the governors asking that the Boarding House be run by himself and his wife in return for free board. The governors decided that they could not agree to this proposal, with the result that Mr Marlar withdrew his acceptance of the post. There followed a protracted period in which Mr Gudgin continued as Acting Head. In March 1946 he was offered the post of Head Master for three years from September 1946. However the Ministry of Education insisted that the post should be properly advertised. Eventually this was done and after four candidates were interviewed in April 1947 Mr Gudgin was finally confirmed as Head Master. The situation had become almost farcical, since Mr Marlar had himself not been the governors' first choice. The post had at first been offered to a Mr Defoe, the Head Master of Queen Elizabeth Grammar School in Kirby Lonsdale, but he had declined it.

In the immediate post-war period, the numbers on roll were fairly static at about 400 to 430. But the numbers taking public examinations did increase. From 5 taking the Higher School Certificate in 1945 the number rose to 19 in 1949 and it was 17 in 1950. However, the pass rate did not rise proportionately. The best results were in 1947 and 1948 when 7 out of 8 and 12 out of 15 passed. In 1949 13 were successful but that was out of an entry of 19 and the following year it was 11 out of 17. There were however 8 Major County Scholarships awarded and 5 of the boys went on to university. Numbers taking School Certificate also went up and there were some pleasing results, for example in 1947 52 passed out of 66 candidates and in 1949 it was 51 out of 62. Although the entry was smaller in 1948, 42 out of 46 were successful, a 91% pass rate, compared with 75% for the country as a whole.

As in the earlier half of the decade, inter-house sport was the mainstay of the extra-curricular programme. The clubs and societies continued to attract supporters, albeit with varying degrees of success at different times. New ones included a Radio Society, started up in 1946, and a Rifle Club in 1949. Both of these had existed for a time in the interwar period. Tennis continued to suffer from logistical problems. In the summer of 1946, for example, play was severely curtailed because no new surround netting could be obtained. However, senior pupils were allowed to play on the Girls' High School courts once per week and twenty-four of them took part in a mixed-doubles tournament in 1946 and that was to become an annual event.

Also on the sporting front, James Gibson (1931-38) was finally awarded a soccer Blue in 1946. He had gone up to Emmanuel College, Cambridge, in 1939 and was selected to play for the University, including the match against Oxford. However it had been decided not to award Blues during the War. In 1940 he joined the navy, resuming his studies in 1946 when he was able to gain

The School House 1st Xl, winners of the inter-house Cricket Shield in 1946

the Blue denied him in 1939. The future England cricketer Peter Parfitt was at K.E.S. from 1945 to 1950, but unfortunately he left to go to Fakenham after only two years in the main school.

It was reported in 1946 that the Musical Society had put on a successful concert and that this 'was probably due to the fact that we did not bring in people from the town to perform. The school orchestra, which has greatly increased in strength, provided most of the concert helped out by solos from members of the school.' This was an interesting comment on previous concerts. The orchestra, trained by Mr Bone, was to provide musical accompaniment at school plays and at Speech Days for several years. In 1949 a Junior Choir also performed at Speech Day. 1946 also saw a return to tradition with the production of *Julius Caesar*, the first Shakespearean play for ten years. *Macbeth, Twelfth Night* and *Richard ll* followed in successive years and in 1950 Mr Cuthbertson produced his penultimate school play, Sheridan's *The Rivals*, a remarkable sequence of successes, going back to 1928. Cuthy's other major responsibility, *The Lennensian*, was severely curtailed in size throughout the 1940s because of the shortage of paper. Often its news was sombre but it also tried to keep a smile on the faces of its readers, for example with more cartoons in the '*As others see us*' series in the December 1946 edition.

With the easing of restrictions, regular trips became a feature of school life, and not just Science Society visits to local firms. In 1950, for example, a group of pupils was taken to Gaywood Park School to see a performance by the Young Vic Players. Fieldwork in geography began in 1947 when Mr Stanley Beaumont led a group of sixth formers on a cycling expedition to collect soil samples and to acquire knowledge of the local area. The new GCE Advanced level syllabus

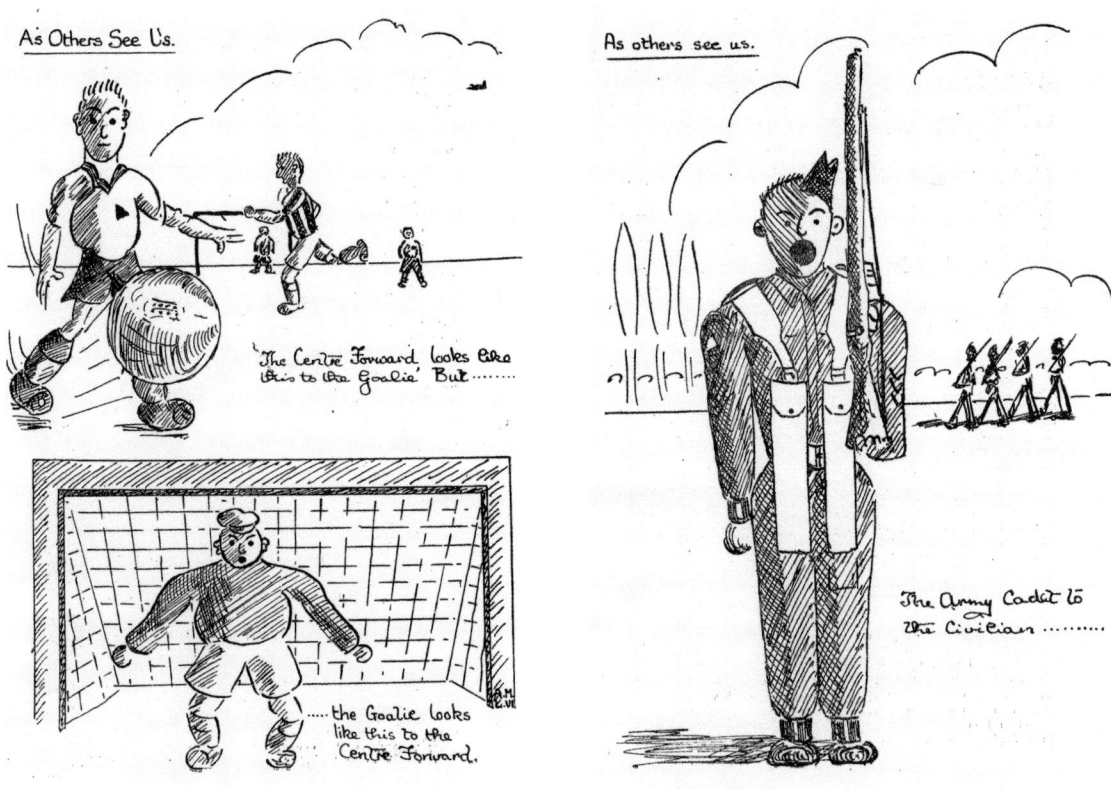

'The centre forward as seen by the goalie' and   The army cadet as seen by civilians'
'the goalie as seen by the centre forward'

specifically emphasised the importance of fieldwork and so in 1950 the intrepid geographers cycled to Scolt Head Island near Blakeney to study the effects of coastal deposition. This was to mark the beginning of many such trips in the second half of the century, although coach and minibus travel would replace the bicycle.

Equally important was the first of many post-war school trips to different parts of Europe. Mr A M Williams, the teacher in charge of French, took a party of 24 boys to Paris and then to Lancieux on the Breton coast for two weeks in August 1950. It clearly made a huge impression on John Vernon (1941-52), who wrote a detailed report on the trip for *The Lennensian*, saying that it 'was the most marvellous holiday and the most invigorating experience.' His comparison between French bread and that available in England, particularly in the 1950s, is one most of us would agree with: 'The British counterpart seemed like bread fish-bait after a fortnight in France.'

The privations of the war years continued, with rationing and shortages in the second half of the decade. Things that seem mundane and even comical today loomed large in the daily life of the school. The Head Master had to take the most simple of decisions to the governors for their approval. For example in June 1947 he had to ask for permission to buy a clock for the kitchen in the Boarding House. At the same meeting he reported the difficulty being experienced in obtaining darning wool for the boarders' clothes. The governors authorised him to ask parents of boarders to provide one clothing coupon for each child so that darning wool could be obtained.

It was also many years before the damage caused by the fire bombing in 1942 was to be properly repaired. Initially, large sheets of tarpaulin were used to cover the roofs and then corrugated-iron sheeting replaced them. A very poignant editorial in *The Lennensian* (Spring 1947) refers to the very harsh winter and the fact that a gale was blowing as the Editor was writing:

> 'Large pieces of our temporary roofing have been stripped off and the night is noisy with the clamour of loosened pieces. Once it was the vast clapping of tarpaulins which disturbed us; now the sheet-iron clatters. It is a sad comment on the complicated state of our land that in an age when the importance of education is emphasised in every way possible to paper and print, a fine school such as ours should be allowed to decay. Five years have passed since the enemy bombs damaged it, but the promised rebuilding seems as remote as we felt it to be on that summer night when we watched the building burning.'

The condition of the buildings was severely criticised in the 1949 Inspection Report by HMI. The fact that there had been only temporary repairs to the science wing, damaged in the air raid in 1942, meant that the condition of the top floor was described as 'deplorable':

> 'The art and biology rooms are without ceilings, cold, dirty, badly lit and barely protected against the weather. The chemistry laboratory on the second floor is without its ceiling, in place of which are visible the fire-blackened beams of the biology room above….Perhaps the most serious of all is the dirty and generally neglected state of almost all the interior decoration of the school. Classrooms, corridors, hall and practical rooms alike appear dismal and dingy, and the evident tolerance of grimy and faded paintwork cannot fail to affect the outlook of the boys. Throughout the building there is an absence of brightness, colour and of any visual background likely to stimulate good taste. In this spacious and well-proportioned building boys could grow up with an appreciation of dignity and refinement…but at present this opportunity is largely lost.'

There were also serious criticisms of some of the teaching and standards of work, especially in religious education, Latin and mathematics. The teaching of mathematics, for example, was described as 'formal, old-fashioned and uninteresting.' Textbooks dominated the teaching and boys practised a large number of techniques without ever being taught their meaning. 'In nearly all classes little deductive work is attempted, the very essence of the subject thereby being avoided.' It did not help that the Senior Mathematics Master, Mr C V Grant, who had joined the school in 1920, was the only graduate in the subject. The other three teachers involved were non-specialists. Another devastating criticism of the mathematics department was that only one of the four teachers regularly collected in work for marking. Instead boys marked their own work in class and so even the ablest boys persisted in serious errors; setting out was clumsy and fallacies and logical absurdities were uncorrected. It is hardly surprising that the governors' sub-committee, set up to consider the HMI Report, interviewed Mr Grant about the criticisms and decided to recommend the appointment of a new Senior Mathematics Master. Unfortunately, a year later in February 1951, the staffing committee had been unable to find suitable candidates either for that post or for one of Senior Science Master, considered necessary because the two most senior science teachers were the Head Master and the Deputy Head Master. It would be yet another year before Mr H Thornton and Mr G A Redhead were appointed. One possible reason for the failure to make these appointments was that the Special Responsibility Allowances paid by the Norfolk Education Authority were lower than those paid elsewhere. It would seem staffing problems have been a problem on and off throughout the school's history.

In the HMI Report, the 'academic equipment' of the staff was described as 'adequate rather than distinguished.' There were two teachers of 'outstanding merit' but the general level was otherwise 'below average in teaching power', though 'effort and good will were rarely lacking.' Some able teaching was seen; but 'often it is dull, uninspired, and fails to stimulate the boys.' The Head Master had been appointed in 1945 'at a time of difficulty for the school'. He had been on the staff for 25 years and 'well past the usual age for undertaking such new and heavy responsibilities, and not unnaturally is not fully conversant with modern scholarship and educational tendencies.' However the Report paid tribute to his unremitting energy, his willingness to take, in emergency, a heavy teaching programme and his loyalty to all concerned in the welfare of the school.

The Report did comment favourably on what extra-curricular activities took place, although it pointed out that there were not many non-sporting activities available: 'The school is active and versatile on the playing fields and supports a flourishing Cadet Corps. Other school societies are well served by the Masters associated with them but they are few in number.' This was partly explained by the fact that large numbers of boys left the school early to catch buses. The Report stated that the Musical Society had long rendered excellent service and that the keenness of its members underlined the need for more effective provision of music in the school. To an extent this statement echoed comments from the Board of Education in 1934, following the last HMI Inspection, although at that time there was virtually no extra-curricular music.

The general attitude of the boys was said to be 'characterised by good humour and persistence rather than by marked enthusiasm.' In social relationships they 'displayed goodwill, often coupled with a distinct reserve and awkwardness.' These characteristics reflected 'the example set before them and the training they receive.' The daily life of the school, the Report said, was 'marked by decorum but not by easy courtesy; on such occasions as morning assembly and the mid-day meal the routine is efficient but there is little inspiration or social grace.' However, the HMI acknowledged that the influence on the boys of the barren and colourless interior of the school should not be under-rated. 'In all, the school is a well-conducted community but not one in which cultural influences are flourishing.'

The general conclusion in the 1949 HMI Report was:

> 'The school is sound at heart and has much steady achievement to its credit, particularly in the examination field, but it is not yet giving its boys full opportunities in any other sphere. The chief needs are for greater intellectual stimulus and more positive cultural and social leadership.'

There were several major ramifications for the school following the 1944 Education Act. In 1947 the Norfolk Education Authority proposed in a development plan that K.E.S. should be a two-form entry, voluntary-controlled school for 360 boys, including 40 boarders. The school would no longer be able to charge fees. A new instrument of government and new articles were introduced in 1948. Also, to the great disappointment of the Head Master and the governors, the Preparatory Department was to be phased out. It had taken boys at age 8 and there were three classes: the Lower Prep; the Upper Prep; and Transition. It was finally closed at the end of the summer term 1950 when the man in charge, Mr G H Martin, teacher at the school for 40 years, retired. George Martin was, according to David Cobbold (1945-53), 'a kindly man and a dedicated teacher, well liked by the boys despite being a strict disciplinarian'. Robert Avis (1928-31) concurs, saying that he 'was a real stalwart of the school, and I am sure was remembered with affection by many pupils'. From September 1942, since his room on the ground floor of the Boarding House was needed because of the damage to the upper floors caused by the fire-bombing, his base became the Old Sanatorium. In the 1950s, this accommodation was used for mathematics and was to be familiarly known in future years as Harry's Hut, named after Harry Thornton.

Another consequence of the 1944 Education Act was that, for the second time in its history, the school might have lost the Royal Gold Medal. In 1948 consideration was given to the fact that the school, under the new Act, had become government controlled and an official at the Privy Purse asked whether it was still appropriate for the King to award a Gold Medal. Captain Fellowes, the Land Agent at Sandringham and a member of the governing body, pointed out in a letter to the Keeper of the Privy Purse, that he had been nominated by the King as a governor, that there was nothing in the new instrument of government which prevented the award and that the school and the Education Authority earnestly hoped that His Majesty would continue to present the medal as before. Fortunately the decision was favourable. A brief hand-written note (dated 24/11/48) on the correspondence which I have seen in the Royal Archive at Windsor states: 'The King has decided to continue to present personally this medal.'

One of the school's major prizes dates from 1950 when Mr Oliver R Jermyn left the very substantial sum of £500 in his will, the interest from which was to be used for an annual prize. Mr Jermyn was an old boy of the school, who had been President of the Old Lennensians' Association in 1935/36 and for many years a governor. The *Oliver Jermyn Prize* was to be awarded 'to the boy who, in the opinion of the Head Master, has shown himself to have made most progress and relatively according to his sphere to have done his best to make himself as proficient as possible.' Just after the end of the War another prize had been donated in memory of Sub-Lieutenant Peter Baillie, who had died of infantile paralysis in Ceylon in 1944. In 1945 his father donated £250 to fund three prizes: a senior piano prize; a junior piano prize; and one for an essay connected with British drama. Today the interest from the investment funds the *Baillie Memorial Senior* and *Baillie Memorial Junior Prizes for Music*.

Mr Sydney Gudgin with staff and Old Boys at the Old Lennensian Rally in the summer of 1951

Mr Gudgin had first joined the staff on a temporary basis in February 1920 to teach science during the illness of the newly-appointed Mr Wagstaff. Hassell Smith remembers him as a good teacher of chemistry 'in a formal and didactic way' and says that he had 'quite a formidable manner.' This is confirmed by Professor Patrick Riley (1946-53) who says that Mr Gudgin was an austere man who rarely ventured out of his study:

> 'He was greatly feared by the young and any stepping out of line in class attracted the instruction to go and report to the headmaster. The technique for survival was to knock extremely quietly on the outer office door and then to find it necessary to make an urgent visit to the lavatories until the bell rang for the next period. On describing this to my father, who was an Old Lennensian himself, I discovered that this practice had a long and distinguished history.'

When he retired in 1951, Sydney Gudgin had been Second Master for twenty-three years and Head or Acting Head for six. As a successful teacher of chemistry, many had passed through his hands, some of whom became 'scientific authorities in the Universities of Oxford and Edinburgh, engineers in oil and light alloys, biologists and doctors.' (*The Lennensian*, July 1951.) At Mr Gudgin's last Speech Day in December 1950, the Chairman of Governors, Alderman J H Catleugh, said that, proof of Mr Gudgin's good work could be judged by the tenor of the 1949 report of H M inspectors which he said was full of praise for him and 'they do not often throw away bouquets.' However, as we have seen, the report did have some damning criticisms which no doubt, at least in part, led to his decision to retire. Tragically he died in January 1952, very soon after his retirement. The school at the beginning of the 1950s was ready for someone with new ideas and the energy to put them into practice. That man was to be Mr A H Sleigh.

5. The Grammar School, 1951-76

Another scientist, this time a biologist, was to follow Mr Gudgin as Head Master. Mr Alan H Sleigh, known to friends as Pat, was to be in charge for twenty-five years, from 1951 to 1976, longer than any other in recent times, with the exception of Walter Boyce. Mr Sleigh had previously been a House Master at Rossall School in Lancashire and, like his counterpart at the beginning of the century, he was a keen cricketer. It was a period in which major changes took place in the school and it became very successful, one of Norfolk's flagship grammar schools.

Mr Sleigh realised that standards of achievement were too low. In October 1952 he highlighted the problem to governors by producing figures showing that the average number of passes in the new GCE 'O' level examination in the A Form was 6.6 in 1951 and 6.0 in 1952, compared with 3.1 and 2.5 respectively in the B Form. Furthermore there was a marked difference between the top ten or so boys in the B Form who achieved four or more passes and the other twenty boys who only got one or even none. In his view about 15% of the intake of 60 boys each year was of too low ability to cope with the grammar school curriculum and he suggested that there should be easier transfer of boys during the first two years to secondary modern schools or to the technical school. He acknowledged that the 11 plus examination was not a good predictor of success since the rank order in the tests bore little relation to future success. This was to be one of the strongest arguments for comprehensive schools in decades to come. It is perhaps ironic that Mr Sleigh, who was to the end a staunch supporter of grammar schools, recognised at this early stage one of the big flaws in the tripartite system of education, brought in by the 1944 Education Act.

As well as problems with the intake there were, according to Mr Sleigh, three other explanations of the low standards: a slackening of effort in the middle years; the promotion of whole forms at the end of each year, irrespective of the progress made by individuals; and the placement of boys into two streams by ability. The effect of the latter, he told governors, was to concentrate 'all the duds' together and they formed 'a hard core' which attracted others. Although streaming by ability was continued in the fourth and fifth years, he decided, as an experiment, not to stream the third year groups, except for Latin and Spanish. He proposed to hold boys back at the end of the year if they had not made enough progress and he introduced a system of *form orders*. Putting the boys into rank order four times each term, based on the marks for each subject, would help form masters monitor the work of individual boys more closely. This system was amended in 1958 when it was decided that form masters would complete report cards three times each term and that these would be sent home. It had been realised that the information was not always being communicated to parents! Unfortunately this system of ranking boys also involved a scaling of marks, which served to emphasise the difference in performance between the different forms. The top groups' marks were scaled from 40 to 80, the middle groups' marks from 20 to 60 and the bottom groups' marks from 0 to 40. In theory therefore boys in the bottom sets could end up with no marks in all their subjects. It is hardly surprising that boys who were in the B and C forms did badly in public examinations. Their low marks presumably discouraged them from trying harder.

In the early 1950s the small number of boys gaining university and state scholarships was also of concern to Mr Sleigh. He felt that not only had there been a lack of appreciation of the importance of such awards by both staff and boys, but also that the bright boys were held back to the pace of the slowest. To counter this he introduced a scheme of accelerated promotion in the first two years and early entry for 'O' level for a number of boys in the fourth form, who would then be able to spend three years in the sixth form. In addition the first sets in the fifth form would do as much sixth-form work as possible to give them a 'flying start' in their 'A' level courses.

Not only were academic standards low at the beginning of the 1950s, but so also were standards of behaviour. Mr Sleigh told the governors that there was a 'lack of tone in the school, shown by lack of interest in such activities as inter-school football, maltreatment of books, dishonesty, petty theft, bullying etc.' He proposed to take a firm line against such poor behaviour. Corporal punishment would be used for bullying and the practice of throwing boys into a holly bush, traditional for many years, was banned. Prefects would ensure good behaviour on buses and trains.

Many old boys from the 1940s and early 1950s remember the tradition, at break time on the first day of term, of throwing new boys into the holly bush situated behind the King's statue. David Morgan (1950-55) describes first years being hurled, one by one, into the prickles of the bush. Shaking with fear and worried about what his new uniform had cost his mother, David clenched his fists and told them they would have to fight him if they wanted to throw him in the bush. He imagines that they took his fear for rage as they moved on to the next boy. He went home with a clean uniform. David recalls Mr Sleigh bringing this particular initiation ceremony to an end early in the 1950s.

Throughout his time Mr Sleigh was a keen disciplinarian and inevitably some students felt they had been unjustly treated on occasions. Perhaps one of the most annoying scenarios was for those who were caned for smoking. Since the Head Master himself was a chain smoker, offenders would watch him put his cigarette down on an ashtray and then pick it up again once he had applied the cane. Robert Edmonds (1955-60) was still annoyed when he recalled, fifty years on, being punished for eating chips out of doors, on the grounds that 'Grammar School boys do not eat chips in the street,' despite the fact that the offence had been committed on a Friday evening at about 6 pm

The Grammar School staff in 1959

when he had already been home and was out of uniform. However Mr Sleigh was quite impartial when it came to using the cane. The punishment book includes an entry for 15 November 1964 when his son, James Sleigh, was caned for 'downright insolence' to a master.

The increase in numbers came rapidly. A change in policy meant that 90 boys rather than 60 were admitted to the first year in 1953. This seems somewhat at odds with the Head Master's view expressed in 1952 that too many boys admitted were not bright enough to cope with the grammar school curriculum. Be that as it may, by 1955 the number on roll had gone up to 470, in 1959 it had reached 550, and by 1963 it had topped 600 for the first time. In part the increase was due to a higher staying on rate at age sixteen. The numbers in the sixth form, which had been very low before the war, went up steadily to 65 in 1954, to over 100 in 1960 and 137 in 1963 when a record 63 boys took GCE Advanced Level examinations. One reason for the increase in numbers in the sixth form was the availability of grants, covering fees and living expenses, to students who were offered places at universities and colleges. Before the war, unless students came from well-off families, they had had to win an Oxbridge, State or Major County Scholarship if they were to be able to afford the cost of going to university.

An HMI Report in October 1957 was very complimentary about what had been achieved since 1949.

> 'The Head Master…has brought to his task a firm determination to raise the standard of the school in every respect, and by his organisation has done much to give opportunity to both the gifted and the less-able boy….the advances that have been made are due largely to his work and enthusiasm.'

By the time of the Report nearly all the criticisms made in 1949, in relation to premises and equipment, had been met. A big improvement in the fabric of the school was finally achieved in 1951 when the roofs damaged by the fire bombing in 1942 were retiled. Further alterations to the Boarding House were carried out. On the top floor the former long dormitory had been sub-divided so there were now Senior, Middle and Junior Dormitories, each sleeping roughly 15 boys. The middle floor had been considerably altered. The former dormitory had been sub-divided into a large house library, a corridor and a House Master's bathroom and storeroom. The original corridor had been divided into three prefects' studies, each normally accommodating two prefects. 'After ten years, life has returned to normal,' it was reported in the summer edition of *The Lennensian* in 1952.

The story was one of continuing improvements, culminating in the opening of a new block in 1956, containing two new classrooms, a biology laboratory, a general science laboratory and a woodwork room. This was built at a cost of £14,500 on the site of the old woodwork room destroyed by fire in June 1953. It was this extension, needed because of the increasing numbers on roll, which the Queen was invited to open in 1956. The visit is recorded by a little-noticed plaque, designed and made in the school, in the entrance to what is now referred to as E Block. A signed photograph of the Queen, which is hanging in the Hall, also commemorates the visit.

The main purpose of the visit, on the 18th January 1956, was to commemorate the fiftieth anniversary of the opening of the school, although the actual date was some ten months off. The Queen drove to the school from Sandringham, accompanied by her Lady in Waiting, the Assistant Private Secretary and the Deputy Master of the Household. She was welcomed by the Lord Lieutenant of Norfolk and the Mayor and Mayoress of King's Lynn. Accompanied by Under Officer Tim Riley (1946-56), Her Majesty inspected the Guard of Honour, provided by the school Cadet

The Queen inspecting the Guard of Honour accompanied by Under Officer Tim Riley

Mr W. H. Beaumont with his French class (EDP)

A memorial plaque was unveiled to commemorate the royal visit in 1956 (Lynn News)

Mr L C Vernon responding to the Queen's questions (Lynn News)

Colin Smith receiving his Gold Medal from the Queen (Lynn News)

The Queen shows an interest in woodwork

Force, unveiled the plaque to commemorate the official opening of the new building, and presented the Gold Medal to 1955 winner, Colin Smith (1948-57). The Queen was presented with a jewellery box by the Head Boy, David Fleming (1945-56). It had been made by the woodwork master, Doug McCall, with the help of a number of boys, from walnut taken from a 150-year-old organ.

The visit was the Queen's last engagement before embarking on an official visit to Nigeria the following week. One of the classrooms visited was a geography lesson in which a film-strip on Nigeria was being shown. In a French lesson the timetable for the Queen's visit had been written on the blackboard, in French of course. There was also a note to the effect that there might be a 'holiday in commemoration of the visit'. Her Majesty obviously took the hint and in a telephone call to the Head Master that evening the Assistant Private Secretary asked that the boys be granted a day's holiday. As well as geography and French lessons, she also saw some history, English, science, craft and PE being taught.

So Colin Smith received his Gold Medal from the Queen in school rather than, as was usual, at Sandringham House. On other occasions too during Mr Sleigh's headship the award was not made at Sandringham House or not by the Queen herself. John Vernon, the son of Mr L C Vernon, in common with the Second World War medallists, was one of the unlucky students not to have his medal presented. Like his father before him, King George Vl showed a very considerate attitude to medallists, as demonstrated by an internal memo to Captain Peter Townshend, the Royal Equerry, in the autumn of 1951. It said that the King would present the medal to John Vernon in the New Year if he was spending his Christmas holiday at home in Lynn, but that if this was not the case he should not be brought home specially. John was due to go to Sandringham on 10 February 1952 to receive the medal from King George Vl but sadly the King died four days earlier. The 1953 winner, Gerald Hamilton (1946-53), received the medal from the Queen Mother at Clarence House, as the Queen was abroad on an official visit. The presentation would have been at Sandringham but Hamilton was in the RAF and his leave was in December when the Royal Family was still in London. Richard Peckover (1953-61), the 1959 winner, was presented with his medal by the Duke of Edinburgh, as the Queen was expecting Prince Andrew. In 1975 and 1976 the presentations to Michael Seaman (1968-74) and Martin Stafford (1968-75) took place at Wood Farm at Wolferton, because major work being carried out at Sandringham House made it impossible for the Royal Family to stay there. On one occasion Mr Vernon, the Deputy Head, accompanied the medallist to Sandringham as Mr Sleigh was in West Africa helping to set up an examinations' syndicate.

To return to buildings, the major deficiencies, once the new block had been completed in 1956, concerned the heating system, the gymnasium and the library. The Head Master told the governors that 'the present gymnasium, small, inconvenient and store less, with its lack of adequate showers and changing rooms, is the least satisfactory part of the premises….The library, too, is small and unattractive, though it will no doubt be improved by the provision of new furniture which is under consideration.' The old heating system was replaced in 1958, allowing, for the first time, hot showers after games and heating in every classroom. The chimney stack which had to be erected did not however enhance the attractiveness of the buildings. In 1969, as numbers continued to grow, a new library and classroom block was built and additional tennis courts and jumping pits were provided on the field.

Mr Sleigh had been arguing the case for additional accommodation for some time. The governors were informed by the Local Education Authority that £20,000 had been included in the estimates for the 1967/68 building programme and the county architect was to draw up plans for a library and additional classroom accommodation. The building was originally planned to be on the land opposite the main door to the hall. It was announced at a governors' meeting that 'the erection of this additional accommodation would mean the removal of the statue to a position beyond the boarding house.' Amazingly no one at the meeting raised any objections. Fortunately objections were raised by the King's Lynn Borough Council to this outrageous suggestion and subsequently it was decided to re-site the new accommodation behind the main building, near the old sanatorium, on what had been the Headmaster's tennis court and vegetable garden. For obvious reasons, the Head Master had favoured the site originally proposed.

One building which has seen several changes of use is the old cadet hut, built in the 1940s on the corner of the field by the Gaywood Road. It was handed over to the sixth form as a common room in 1969 and a great deal of work was involved in installing a ceiling and decorating it. Unfortunately, as is often the case, the freedom enjoyed by all in the common room was abused by the minority and the work of redecoration had to be done again a year later. In June 1971 its use by the sixth form was brought to an end. A year later the Head Master was describing it as a white elephant. Its use as a music room was briefly considered but then abandoned.

'Many of the staff are generous with their time in fostering and helping with out-of-school activities.' (HMI Report, 1957.)

Even in 1952 the Head Master could report that there were ten clubs and societies holding regular meetings and there were also weekly classes in ballroom dancing and square dancing held jointly with students from the King's Lynn Girls' High School. Throughout his time Mr Sleigh actively promoted a wide range of extra-curricular activities.

Mr Sleigh supervising the rolling of the cricket square, his pride and joy

In particular he did much to support the sporting aspect of school life. Both individuals and teams had considerable success. James Sleigh (1962-69), the Head Master's younger son, excelled in two different sports, hockey and cricket. He played hockey for the county for several years and captained Norfolk in 1968-69. In cricket he also captained the county 1st XI and played in matches between the North and South of England. James was also selected to play in an English Schools' Cricket XI, although the match against the Canadian Cricket Colts at Ilford in 1970 was abandoned due to heavy rain. He did however play for Cambridge against Oxford and toured Canada as Vice-Captain of a combined Oxford and Cambridge team. He was the school's first Hockey Blue and only the third Blue since WW1. The only other two were Football Blues: George Way in 1931/32; and James Gibson in 1946.

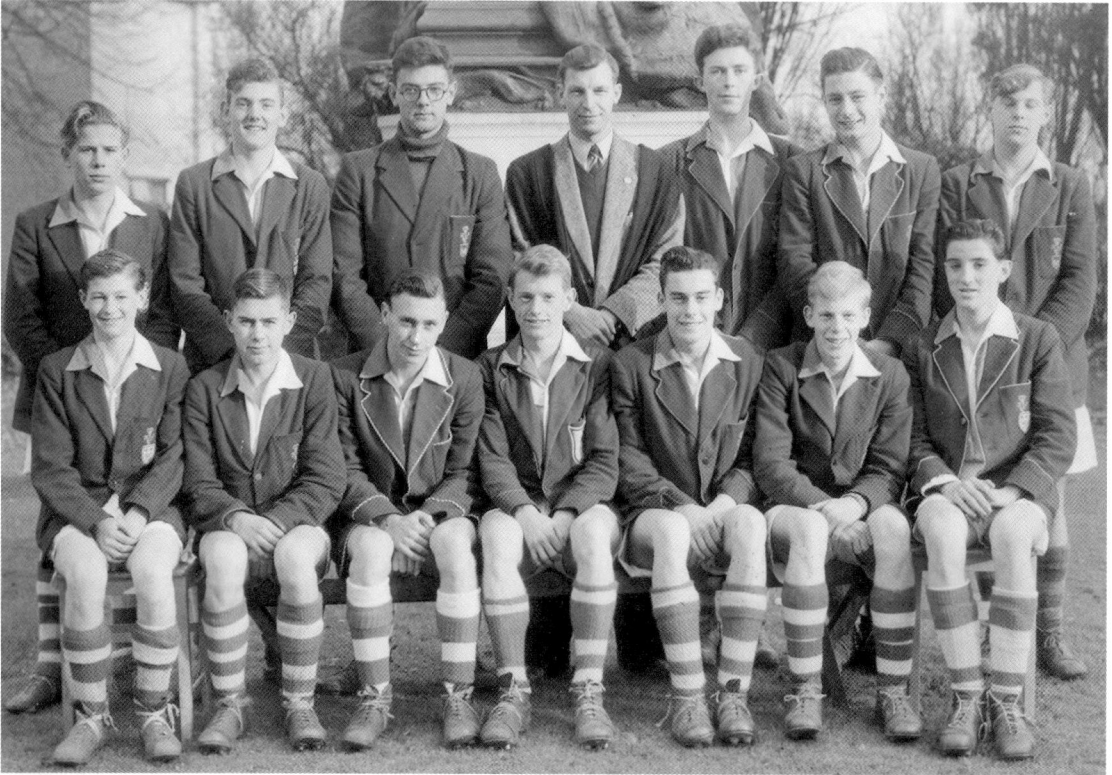

The 1955-56 1st XI Football team with Mr K. B. Gregory

Perhaps the most outstanding sportsman of the 1970s was Ken Gregory's elder son Tim (1967-74). While still at school he played in an English Schoolboys' Hockey side in a triangular international tournament at Weybridge in April 1974 and his performance was commended in the national press. Gregory was also selected for the U21 England Hockey Squad and in 1975 played in an International Tournament in Barcelona. In 1976 he was capped seven times at U21 level and played in goal for a Europe U21 team against the Dutch Olympic side. Having captained the England U21 team throughout the 1977 season he graduated to the full England side and went on to play many times for his country.

Other notable sportsmen while at school include Bob Childs (1966-72) who played and captained Norfolk at U15 and U19 level as well as appearing in matches for the South of England against the North (run by the English Schools Cricket Association) and the North v the South (in matches run

The 1970-71 1st Xl Football team with Mr D. G. Register

The 1958-59 1st Xl Cricket team with Mr C. M. Bayfield.

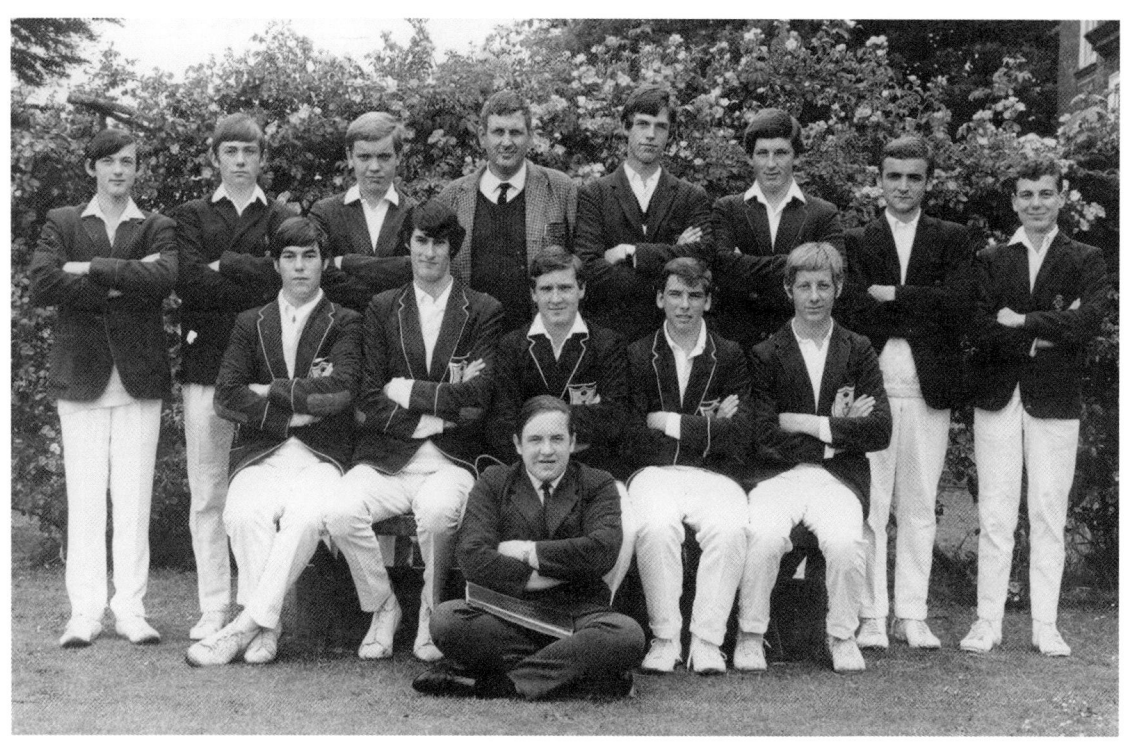

The 1968-69 1st Xl Cricket team with Mr J. P. Smallwood

The 1959-60 2nd Xl Hockey team with Mr J. S. Upcher

The 1968-69 School Hockey team with Mr D. Whitmarsh-Knight

by the National Association of Young Cricketers.) At Hove in August 1971 he played for the North against a team from the South which included a young Graham Gooch.

Mention must also be made of Alex Macduff (1964-71) who excelled in athletics and was selected to play at county and regional levels, reaching the national standard in the high jump from 1966 onwards.

The outstanding success at national level for a team came in 1975 when the U15 Cricket team reached the final of the Lord's Taverners Competition at the Oval. Unfortunately the team lost to Radley College by 42 runs. An article in *The Lennensian*, 1974/75 tells the story:

'A thousand miles of mini-bus travel, a night's sojourn in a reputedly haunted North Wales Youth Hostel, interminable net practices, breath taking finishes, and ultimately every schoolboy cricketer's dream of playing at the hallowed Oval wicket – these were some of the memories of a remarkable summer term for our Under 15 team….There will be many explanations for our defeat; perhaps our quick bowlers lost their edge after such a taxing summer; perhaps the occasion affected our team more than Radley's, which contained four players with experience of the previous year's final….The post mortem revealed that marginal umpiring decisions cost us dearly…..In spite of the result this was a magnificent day in the school's history, finalists out of the original entry of 943 schools, and one which the players and our wonderful enthusiastic supporters will long remember.'

'The Oval Boys' - runners up in the 1975 Lords Taverners' competition with coach, Ken Gregory

Above: Pat Cooke receiving his runners-up medal; Ian Grady, Chris Nelson, Steve Bunting and David Bird looking on

Left: Steve Bunting and David Bird going out to open the batting at the Oval

Teams were also successful at county level, for example in 1973 the U15 team won the Scott Chad Cup.

The U15 winners of the Scott Chad Cup in 1973 with Mr J C Grinham.

Not everyone was keen on sport, especially swimming. David Sandford (1959-66) recalled walking through the fog to the outdoor swimming pool by the groundsman's shed:

'The pool was still being filled from the mains, a four-inch pipe at the shallow end. Teeth chattering, having changed under what resembled a bike shelter, we were expected to line up at the side of the pool in order of height. *In, under and out*' was the single instruction before the whistle blew. Was he serious? I was a complete non-swimmer. He was serious. The water was so cold it took the last breath of air from your lungs.'

There was certainly plenty of amusement to be had after the 'A' level examinations had finished in 1971. Sixth formers organised a Rag Week which must go down as one of the most successful fund-raising events in the school's history, if not in terms of the money raised, certainly in terms of the range of activities and the enjoyment generated. It all started at 5 am on Sunday 11 July when the school was decorated with bunting and, to the annoyance of the Head of PE, a tracksuit was flown from the flag pole. The events included a car rally, a staff versus students tug of war, a 'poets' cornered' competition, a sponsored silence, an all-night darts marathon, an attempt to break the egg throwing and catching record, a boggart hunt and a wheelbarrow obstacle race. The photograph of the wheelbarrow race is a splendid reminder of that week in 1971. It shows the winners, Alan Middleton pushed by Brian White, flanked on the left by Ian Stockwell and Andrew Bridle and on the right by Peter King and Dick Waite. Max Finbow, in pyjamas, and Michael Perryman lead the supporters. Other events included Mike McDonnell, known as 'Elmer' because of his American

For once masters let themselves be pushed about by their pupils – this wheelbarrow race was one of the activities in the K.E.S. Rag Week, July 1971 (Lynn News)

connections, gamely allowing himself to be put in the stocks to be coated with custard and also attempting the world roundabout circumnavigation record! An attempt to break the walking-backwards record and a twenty-four hour cricket match played to 1770 rules were claimed as two world records. The walking-backwards record was believed at the time to be 32 miles and this was broken by two boys, sixth former Paul Harvey and fourth former Steven Clark, who covered 35 miles. In all some £375 was raised and divided between three charities - Shelter, the St Raphael Club in Gaywood and the Norfolk Fund for the Blind. A good time was had by all.

From the 1950s school trips, at home and abroad, became a regular part of the extra-curricular programme. Over the years there have been many trips to France, including exchange visits with schools at Brive, Compiègne, Paris, Marseilles and Charoux, south of Poitiers. The Brive exchange was longest lasting. It was established by Mr Alan Williams in 1961 and, although it only lasted for five years in the 60s, it was re-established in 1976 and continued until the 1990s. There were many other trips abroad, such as those to Nice, Grenoble, Biarritz, Thonon-les-Bains, Heidelberg, and Lugano. Ray Woodcock (1950-58) describes the trip to the French Riviera in 1958 as 'out of this world.' Walking holidays to the Lake District, the Peak District, the Yorkshire Dales, Snowdonia, Scotland and Ireland, were regular events in the 1960s and 1970s. Field trips in geography and biology, some of them abroad, such as that to Ireland in 1961, are of long standing. In the 1950s the annual trip to Scolt Head Island was almost a pilgrimage. In later years popular centres for geographers included the Yorkshire Dales and the Lake District. The School Prize for Geography dates from 1952 when one of the school's long-serving governors, H G Winearls, left £100 in his will to fund a prize.

Drama was stronger at the beginning of Mr Sleigh's headship than it was in the later years. Since 1928 C E Cuthbertson had produced a play nearly every year. However his last production, in 1952, was *Henry V* and he died in 1954 during preparations for the annual inspection of the Combined Cadet Force, for which he had become, once again, the Adjutant. What kind of a man was Charles Cuthbertson? Old boys' memories are always coloured by their own particular experiences. David Cobbold (1945-53) recalls staff such as him being cold and aloof: 'I cannot recall him ever smiling; one of the unbending masters, although he was a good teacher.' He remembers being set an essay on *Changes I would like to make to school life* and among other things denouncing the strict discipline which he felt characterised the school. The comment on this piece of writing from Cuthy was: 'A boy is not always the soundest judge of what is good for him.' Jim Bridgement (1936-41) saw him in a different light. 'To me, *Cuthy* was K.E.S. I was always in awe and slight fear of his mastery of the English language, but also knew of his real concern for the welfare of the pupils.' When he died on 26 May 1954, after 27 years on the staff, he had made an outstanding contribution to the life of the school as Senior House Master, Senior English Master, producer of school plays, organiser of school trips and visits and as Editor of eighty copies of *The Lennensian*.

In the 1950s and1960s some ambitious musical productions were put on, jointly with the Girls' High School, and staged at the King's Lynn Guildhall. They included *Trial by Jury, Iolanthe, HMS Pinafore, The Gondoliers* and *Penny for a Song*. In 1964 Mr Ken Gregory produced *Henry lV Part 2*, the first Shakespeare play for over ten years. There were also productions of *Dr Faustus, The Private Secretary, The Comic Mask, Dotheboys Hall, Reluctant Heroes* and *Under Milk Wood*. For a few years in the 1970s however, drama went through a bad patch. When productions were staged in 1976 involving first and second year boys, Mr Sleigh told the governors that this revival of interest in dramatic productions was heartening and he hoped it would spread to the higher forms in the near future.

The 1954 production of Iolanthe at the Femoy Centre

As in earlier years, boarders with an interest in music often formed their own groups and practised together in their dining hall where they had the use of a piano. Patrick Riley (1946-53) tells below of the formation of the Jazz Band in 1952:

'Then I discovered Jazz. I first heard it on a scratchy Ladnier-Mezzrow recording but quickly found the exciting sound of Sidney Bechet and later Benny Goodman. My indulgent parents bought me a clarinet and, as the teacher who was to instruct me had had all his teeth extracted and was unable to play, I became an autodidact using Otto Langey's fine *Tutor for the Clarinet and Corno di Bassetto*. Tim was persuaded to play the cornet and soon we had the core of a small band which practised in the Dining Hall. My very sporting aunt underwrote the expense of some ancillary instruments such as a banjo and a bass drum....The musical efforts of the band were not universally applauded and most of the masters, whose common room was situated opposite the main door to the Dining Hall, were careful to keep the intervening doors closed. We did have a temporary junior housemaster, I think by the name of Price, who played very well in the style of Fats Waller but he did not condescend to play with us and we were too timid to approach him.'

The KES Jazz Band 1952

The photograph shows Tim Proffitt (washboard & drums), Patrick Riley (clarinet), Tim Riley (cornet) and Roger Hall (piano, violin & banjo). The group also included Michael Evans who featured prominently in a vinyl acetate recording made in 1953.

During this period several clubs and societies were formed which encouraged the mixing of Grammar School boys and girls from the High School. In 1956-57 an Inter-sixth form Society, also known as the 30-30 Club, was formed and this continued right through to 1968 and beyond, although it was better attended in some years than others. There were social events, talks, debates and film shows. In 1957-58 High School girls attended meetings of the Grammar School Jazz Club. From 1958-59 there was also a Ballroom Dancing Club which was held at the Grammar School until 1963-64 when it was transferred to the High School. A Reels Club at which Scottish Dances were taught by Mr R A 'Monty' Hales at the Grammar School on Saturday evenings was popular for a couple of years in the late 1950s. Ray Simpson (1953-60) says that the 'Reels Club was brilliant. These were the days when girls sat out at dances until asked, whereas reels involved everyone with lots of partner changing and some degree of physical contact. What more could you want, and in the school hall!' Ray met his wife Diana (Buck) at the Reels Club and they have been married for over 50 years.

The Army Cadet Force, originally formed by Mr Hatton in the summer of 1942, continued to be an important feature of the school in the 1950s. In 1951 there was an increase in the Cadet Contingent as a result of the introduction of an RAF platoon. Enthusiasm for the CCF comes through strongly in the following passage sent to me by Ray Woodcock (1950-58):

'The best day of the week after I had reached the age of thirteen was Thursday – this was 'Cadet Afternoon'..... We all spent the first year in the Army cadets learning basic infantry skills and then opted either for the Army or Air Force section. Our instructors in drill, map-reading, tactics and wireless procedure were the senior boys who held the ranks Cadet Corporals and Sergeants. Our officers were some of the masters who wore their reservists' uniforms. Remember this was the 1950s – the Second World War had only been over for a few years and many of the masters had WWII medals and campaign ribbons whilst the younger ones would have done a two-year period of National Service. We drilled under the command of a Cadet Sergeant Major with real Lee Enfield .303 rifles and marched on parade to the bugles and drums of our own band led by a swaggering Cadet Drum Major Geoff Bocking.

I learnt how to iron my khaki shirt, my battledress blouse and my trousers so my uniform was always immaculately creased. My webbing belt and gaiters with their brass buckles were carefully blancoed and polished whilst my boots and hat badge shone in any sunshine. We proudly wore the Britannia hat badge of the Royal Norfolk Regiment in our navy berets with the regimental yellow lanyard on our battledress blouse.

We occasionally had a full day of cadet training when we would go to a range and fire our rifles or spend the day in the nearby Wootton Woods practising tactics and firing blank rounds.…My Cadet training stood me in very good stead when I joined the Territorial Amy in 1961 and later when I was commissioned into the Regular Army in 1965.'

Ray Woodcock (1950-58)

Towards the end of the decade the situation changed with the announcement by the government that National Service would cease in 1960. The value of a school cadet force had to be re-evaluated and in March 1958 Mr Sleigh reported to the governors that, as from the end of the summer term, the activities of the school Cadet Force would no longer form part of the school curriculum. The decision to disband it was taken in 1959 after numbers had fallen considerably and some key staff were about to leave.

The Air Cadet Corps in 1954

By co-incidence, Mr Hatton retired in 1959 after nearly forty years at the school. He had been Second Master since 1945. David Cobbold says that he was "feared by boys as a tough disciplinarian' but 'was nevertheless a good physics master who got good results as boys worked well at his subject.' John Frost (1939-44) would certainly agree with the latter statement. He saw him as a 'great guy' who prompted him to train as a science teacher. One amusing story from the past about Freddie Hatton is told by Bob Booth (1950-58) whose father and his two brothers, in turn, worked as laboratory technicians before the Second World War. Bob's uncle Bill recalls being sent by Mr Hatton, in the late 1920s, to deliver a note to a lady friend and being given a shilling. Mr Hatton was somewhat taken aback when Bill Booth returned and told him he had given the lady the note and the shilling. Hatton told the messenger that he was a 'bloody fool.' It is not known what the lady thought about being given the money!

W H Beaumont, who taught French, also retired in 1959, having been on the staff for thirty-six years. He had served in the Second World War and, according to John Sleigh (1962-69), one of his regular put-downs to potential trouble-makers was: 'I've killed better Germans than you.' John Oddy (1943-50) describes him as 'a distinctive personality' whose lessons were 'so systematic.' French was one of the few subjects John liked until his sixth form years which he found both congenial and rewarding. For many years Beaumont regularly contributed to *The Lennensian* under the pseudonym Uncle Cedric and these pieces of poetry and prose were published by The Witley Press (1960) in a short book, entitled *Dear Boys*, which was dedicated 'To all Lennensians past and present.'

Another long-serving member of staff was C A 'Pop' Freestone who retired in December 1954, after twenty-five years at the school as the Physical Education Master and Keene House Master. 'A real gentleman, well-liked and respected', according to Lionel Jackson (1936-41), while a 1952 leaver describes him as 'always so full of energy and liked by all.' From 1932 he had organised an annual gymnastics display including the competition for the Dennick Cup. He was also the Commanding Officer of the local Air Training Corps and from 1946 had been involved in local politics, becoming Mayor in 1952/53.

Tom Bromhead, who had joined the staff in 1921, after losing an arm in the First World War, retired in 1955 and is remembered with respect by many, especially from the 1930s and 40s. George Hern (1937-42) thought him 'a most conscientious and civilised man' and Keith Banyard (1941-46) says he 'was very much the gentleman who after inflicting some form of punishment on a pupil then proceeded to apologise profusely.' Hassall Smith describes him as 'a fine man whose devotion to his job was as outstanding as it had been to his country. He was not a gifted teacher but I at least responded to his humanity and sincerity.' He also makes the point that, as Windsor House Master, 'no matter what the weather was like, he was always on the touchline encouraging his various teams.'

How successful was this period in the Grammar School's history? Mr Sleigh took over in 1951, the year in which the new system of G.C.E. Ordinary and Advanced levels, replaced the School Certificate and Higher School Certificate. The new 'O' level was equivalent to a credit in the old School Certificate. In 1951 only 17 boys achieved two or more passes at 'A' Level and 34 pupils passed in five or more subjects at 'O' Level. Over the next few years results were not good. For example in 1954 only 9 boys were successful in gaining two or more 'A' Levels. However by 1961 the Head Master was able to report significant progress. The school roll had gone up from 350 to 560, including a rise from 30 to over 100 in the sixth form. In 1961 22 boys had been awarded County Major Scholarships, in addition to 4 State Scholarships and an Oxford Exhibition. Some 45 had achieved passes in two or more subjects at 'A' Level and 53 boys had gained five or more 'O' Levels, including 10 from the fast stream in the 4th Year.

The most successful set of Advanced level results during Mr Sleigh's time as Head Master was in 1973. Of the 56 candidates entered, 45 passed in two or more subjects, the same number as in 1961, but the overall pass rate was up from 71.6% to 80.9%. Some 27 students gained entry to universities, including a record seven to Oxbridge, and a further six were offered places at polytechnics. 14 students, more than twice the normal number, gained the grades to qualify as Norfolk Scholars, that is at least two A grades or one A and two Bs.

But results did fluctuate from year to year. 1974, for example, was a disappointing year for both Advanced level and Ordinary level results. Although the pass rate at Advanced level was 77%, the number of top grades was low and there were many E grades, especially on the Arts side where only three of the students gained university places. The situation was somewhat better in the Sciences but even so only 9 students were offered places at university. At Ordinary level Mr Sleigh reported to the governors that 'a disturbingly large number of boys passed in only three, two or one subject.' He put this down in part to the raising of the school-leaving age to 16 as from 1 September 1973. He felt that the presence of some who might otherwise have left had 'infected several other boys with their own attitudes.' In fact the percentage of boys achieving 5 or more passes was 73.5%, a great deal better than in 1971, for example, when the figure was as low as 59%, and nearly twice the number achieved only three, two or one pass as was the case in 1974.

In his last report to the governors, on the 1976 examinations, Mr Sleigh expressed disappointment that some boys, who had done well in their 'O' levels two years previously, had not been as successful at 'A' level. Nevertheless the pass rate was 77.2% and there were six Norfolk scholars, about the norm for the previous five or six years. He could certainly be pleased with the 'O' level results which were better than they had been for some time: the number gaining five or more passes was up to 70, 84% of the year group.

In the twenty-five years that Mr Sleigh was Head Master, students went on to university in larger numbers than ever before. They also went on to play a part in every walk of life and in every part of the country and abroad. To a much greater extent than before the War the Grammar School was preparing its pupils for a national and international job market. Many Old Lennensians from that era have been very successful in the professions, in academia, in industry, in business, in the armed forces and in the media. To mention just a few examples, Tony Crowfoot (1945-54), the 1954 Gold

Mr Sleigh and his prefects in 1965

Medallist, achieved the rank of Major General in the Army, Patrick Riley (1946-53) became Professor of Cell Pathology at University College, London, Tim Oliver (1954-60) the Sir Maxwell Joseph Professor of Medical Oncology at Bart's and London Hospitals, Michael Smith (1958-65) Professor of European Politics at Loughborough University and, from 2015, Warwick University, Michael Perryman (1965-72) Professor of Astronomy at the University of Leiden in the Netherlands, and Tony Williams (1958-65), a successful solicitor in Lynn, was appointed a Deputy Lieutenant of Norfolk in 2003.

A nostalgic view of the south face of the school in 1973 (EDP)

Another former student who was to have a career in the law was Peter Jacobs (1954-61). Although he originally read history at University College, Cardiff, and taught for a time, he became involved in Liberal Party politics and was sponsored for Grays Inn by Emlyn Hooson QC. After being called to the Bar in 1973 he had a successful career as a barrister before being appointed a circuit judge in 1997. He became the Resident Judge at Norwich Crown Court in 2004, Recorder of Norwich in 2007 and a member of the Court of Appeal Criminal Division in 2008. He retired in 2013 but since then has been Chairman of the Metropolitan Police Independent Advisory Committee on undercover policing and corruption. Very importantly for K.E.S. Peter has been President of the Old Lennensians' Association since 2006.

Mr Sleigh was a somewhat controversial figure. He certainly held strong views and sometimes this caused friction. One of the ongoing debates was about the continuation of Saturday-morning school. He was very much in favour but eventually the opposition was too strong and it ended as from the beginning of the autumn term in 1972. Earlier that year the decision had finally been taken at a meeting of the governors at which the Divisional Education Officer had reminded them of the six occasions between 1950 and 1970 when the question had been discussed. In 1967 parents' views had been sought and, despite a strong case being put by the Head Master, the result was evenly balanced: 95 in favour and 91 against. Mr Sleigh had argued that the results at both 'O' level and 'A' level were better at K.E.S. than comparable schools, most of which did not have Saturday-morning school. He also felt that games and other extra-curricular activities would suffer if it was ended. Following the distribution of a leaflet by a small group of sixth formers at the 1968/69 Prize Giving, complaining about a number of issues including Saturday-morning school, the views of parents and older pupils were again canvassed. This time only 106 parents were in favour compared with 237 against, with 42 having no strong feelings. Of the older pupils consulted only 67 were in favour, 179 against and 18 abstained. Despite this strength of feeling the governors at their June 1970 meeting voted 9 to 4 to retain Saturday-morning school. But the tide had begun to turn.

One positive outcome of the decision to end Saturday-morning school was the introduction of The Duke of Edinburgh Award scheme in 1972, since it was felt that the boarders would benefit from more activities to occupy their time. The governors provided a grant of £150 for the purchase of equipment. Over the years the scheme has waxed and waned but still survives today.

September 1972 was also the date from which the traditional maroon flannel blazer was replaced by a navy-blue barathea blazer with a detachable badge. It was felt that this would be less expensive and more durable. The fact that the badge could be removed also meant that a student would be able to wear the blazer when he left school.

Change was clearly in the air in the early 70s. 1973 saw another break with tradition when Richard Griffiths was appointed Deputy Head. This was the first time that an external appointment had

Mr A H Sleigh together with Mr Bayfield, Mr Hatton, Mr Vernon, and Mr Griffiths, the four Deputy Heads during his twenty-five years as Head Master

been made. In all Mr Sleigh had four Deputies. The others were: F H Hatton (1946-59), L C Vernon (1959-69) and C M Bayfield (1969-73), all of whom had been internally promoted. Mention has already been made above of Freddie Hatton. L C Vernon, whose nickname was inevitably *Elsie*, was an expert on the history of the school and had written an account for the special 25th anniversary edition of *The Lennensian* in 1931. John Oddy, who particularly enjoyed history in the sixth form, says Mr Vernon 'easily combined gravitas with approachability' and Mark Buxton (1967-74) refers to him as 'a lovely gentleman.' Hassell Smith, who went on to become Professor of History at the University of East Anglia, says, 'I owe a great deal to him…..If anyone prepared me for university life it was *Elsie*.'

'Bunny' Bayfield had been a pupil at the school, going up to Emmanuel College, Cambridge, in 1926. As mentioned in Chapter 3, he had been an excellent sportsman at school and he continued to play cricket at a good standard into his fifties. After a career in the Colonial Service he returned to Lynn and joined the staff as a teacher of mathematics in 1955. Mark Buxton says that Bayfield, 'in spite of his fearsome appearance….was a popular member of staff because not only was he an excellent teacher…but he cared about the school and the boys.' John Sleigh supports this assessment: 'With a fearsome, booming voice he had a soft centre and an ability to get his message across better than anyone else.' John tells the story of Bayfield betting all comers in a local hostelry that there would be two customers in the pub with the same date of birth. He won his bet and revealed that in every class of thirty there would always be two boys with the same birthday, so with forty or so people in the pub it was unlikely that he would not find the same.

An important educational change came in 1973-74 with the raising of the school leaving age to 16, generally known as ROSLA. You might have thought that this would not have had a major effect on grammar schools where the clear intention was that students should all stay at school until 16 and take GCE 'O' levels. However in 1974 Mr Sleigh announced the introduction of a new course in the fourth form, involving fewer examination subjects for those 'unwilling or unable to cope with the main offering.' The raising of the school-leaving age was also a major reason given for his decision to introduce a pastoral care system as from September 1974, one of the most controversial issues of Mr Sleigh's time. The year system has in fact become a great strength of the school. However, at the time it was strongly opposed by some who felt that it devalued the existing system based on houses. Perhaps even more controversial was the fact that the *year masters* were appointed without open competition and this caused a great deal of bitterness among some of the staff. There were complaints and deputations to the governors and Mr Sleigh had to agree to consult more widely in future.

By 1956 the numbers in the Boarding House had gone above the nominal capacity of 48 and the Head Master had therefore suggested the purchase of a house opposite the school. This was agreed to by the LEA. However, by the late 1960s and early 70s the decline in numbers had become a constant source of worry. Relatively few boys were joining the school as boarders at age 11 and in June 1968, when it was thought that only one new boy would join in September, compared with eight or nine who were due to leave, the Head Master suggested to the governors that they should close the Boarding House from 1972. However, they were not willing even to consider the possibility at this stage. In 1972 the County Treasurer advised the school that the fees, which had been at £160 per year since 1957, should be increased. Obviously there was concern that an increase might have a further detrimental effect on numbers. Nevertheless, fees were raised to £193 per year in 1973. Mr Sleigh again seemed keen to see the Boarding House closed and reported to governors that the numbers could be down to 30 in September and this would make it uneconomic

School House in 1954

to run. Then the LEA, in 1975, proposed that the Boarding House should be closed as from 1977. However the governors successfully argued that no decision should be taken until the future of the school, in the plans for secondary re-organisation, had been decided.

Discussions on proposals for the re-organisation of education in King's Lynn had taken place as early as 1971. The Western Area Divisional Executive had put forward a plan whereby K.E.S. would become a sixth-form college and the other schools in the area would be 11- 16 comprehensives. Even teachers at the school were divided on this plan. The majority were in favour of some schools becoming 11-16 but wanted K.E.S to be a 14-18 school, taking pupils at 14 who wanted to stay on to 18. This would largely have preserved an academic intake for the school. In the end neither the sixth-form college proposal nor the alternative was implemented by the LEA.

John Sleigh, in an assessment of his father's period as Head Master, believes that his aim was to create a boarding-grammar school to compare with public schools in terms of academic achievement, sport and clubs. One possible mistake, according to John, was that Mr Sleigh took on the role of careers master. He channelled as many boys as possible to university or into teacher training, 'sometimes regardless of suitability and vocation' and 'as a last resort introductions to local solicitors, accountants and surveyors could be made. If all this failed there were one or two commercial organisations known to him that offered training facilities or else it was a matter of being left to one's own devices.' Although Mr Sleigh had seen the school transformed during his time, when he retired in 1976, with comprehensive education inevitable, he felt there was no lasting legacy by which he would be remembered.

Bunny Bayfield in a tribute to Mr Sleigh in *The Lennensian* (1976) felt he was a misunderstood man:

'I knew his four predecessors, having been a pupil of three….Without decrying their achievements none gave more of himself for the school than did Mr Sleigh. He came to a school still showing scars of war and quickly displayed his ability to get things done. Numbers grew from 450 to more than 600. Administrative requirements became more demanding but Mr Sleigh took them in his stride and shaped the school as he thought good. He had his critics, but what man of positive qualities has not? I have often thought that they lacked appreciation of the complex task of a Headmaster who has so many groups and interests to serve. Never did Mr Sleigh attempt to be all things to all men….He always knew what sort of school he wanted and he laboured unremittingly to that end. The Honours Boards, the Record of the school Teams, the high standard of the pitches and last but not least – and this was very close to his heart – the success of the less academically gifted in finding good employment in the locality, are a measure of his achievement.'

Mr Sleigh died in 1994 at the age of 83. At that time, John Smallwood (1959 to 2001) was quoted in the *EDP* as saying:

'Pat was a headmaster of the old school who demanded the highest standards from staff and pupils alike. If a few found him uncompromising in his expectations, many more speak with ungrudging respect both for Pat himself and for the school in which they either spent their formative years or served as teachers. Above all they remember his devotion to the school and the pride he took in its achievements.'

It is clear that in the early years Pat Sleigh did what was necessary to raise standards of achievement and of behaviour in the school. When he left, the school was much more successful than it had been when he arrived. By the end of his headship he was a somewhat disappointed man who felt that much of what he had achieved in the school would be lost in the coming changes. Perhaps he stayed too long in post. The era of comprehensive schools was about to dawn in Norfolk and a different kind of man would be needed to turn what had been a successful boys' grammar school into an equally successful all-ability school for both boys and girls.

6. The Comprehensive Era

Mr R. D. Greaves, Head Master 1976-89

Mr R D Greaves joined K.E.S. at a crucial time in its history. Plans for comprehensive re-organisation had been mooted since the early 1970s and it is hardly surprising that Mr Sleigh's successor was someone with relevant experience. He was the first Head Master to join the school from the state sector rather than from a public school and he had been involved in reorganisation at his previous school in Yeovil. No doubt this was very much in the mind of governors and the LEA when the appointment was made. Certainly Mr Greaves accepted the post on the understanding that the LEA was committed to the school becoming comprehensive. Mr Sleigh had been a man of the old school, an upholder of tradition and someone who had tried to hold back the tide of change sweeping through education, at least within the microcosm of K.E.S. His successor was to introduce major changes in the ethos and direction of the school.

The particular form that comprehensive reorganisation was to take in King's Lynn was finally decided in 1978, after several years of debate. There were to be three mixed high schools, all with sixth forms. For K.E.S. big changes lay ahead, not least the doubling of the size of the school and the massive building programme that was therefore needed. It had also been decided that the Boarding House would be phased out and boarding provision in the county would be concentrated at Wymondham College. Some people, parents, students and staff alike, clearly regretted the end of selection. In June 1979, after Margaret Thatcher's election victory, there was a last-ditch attempt to thwart the impending changes, with letters to the local newspapers, petitions to the County Council and a public meeting. However, by this stage the plans were too far advanced and, in any case, Norfolk was 80% along the way to completing its re-organisation plans which had begun five years earlier.

The catchment area of each high school in Lynn was delimited in such a way as to give each one a roughly equal share of the different socio-economic areas in the town and the surrounding villages. The aim was to ensure that, as far as possible, each school had the chance to develop a fully comprehensive intake. The designated catchment area for K.E.S. included the town wards of St Margaret's, Lynn South West and Chase, as well as the Woottons. From the beginning David Smith, the new Head of Lower School, in an effort to ease the transfer of children from primary to secondary school, established excellent links with the partner schools, Eastgate, Greyfriars and Whitefriars in the town and the two schools in the Woottons.

For some teachers at the school the bigger change from 1979 was not so much the switch to an all-ability entry as the fact that the intake included girls as well as boys. It must also have been a difficult time for the 125 first-year girls in 1979. The twelve young ladies in the sixth form were perhaps happier with the situation in which they found themselves. To cope with the new mixed intake it was important that the make-up of the staff should change and it did. In 1976, when Mr

Greaves took over, there were no female teachers but by September 1979 just over a third of the teaching staff were women, including one of the three deputy heads, Mrs Pat Gregson. She left in 1987 to be replaced by Mrs Kate Wadlow who, together with Richard Griffiths and John Smallwood, were my Deputies when I took over in 1990.

Reorganisation meant upheaval in more ways than one. The existing secondary schools in Lynn were closed and the new ones came into being on 1 September 1979. All the posts in the new schools were advertised and staff had to submit formal applications. Although most stayed in the same school there was some movement between institutions, for example, Tony Wilmore, an Old Lennensian, who had been Head of Chemistry in the Grammar School, was appointed Head of Sixth Form at the new Springwood High School. It was Alan Middleton, the highly-talented teacher of Spanish, who was to obtain that post at K.E.S. He deserves much of the credit for building up the sixth form at a time when there was talk in the

First-year girls arriving in September 1979 at what had been the dayboys' entrance. (EDP)

A new experience for Mr McCall: helping girls in a woodwork lesson in 1979 (Lynn News)

The three Deputy Heads in 1979: Pat Gregson; John Smallwood; and Richard Griffiths

A link with the past: the Head Master and Head Boy, David Wright, talking in 1979 to Osbert Lancaster, the celebrated cartoonist and writer and grandson of the school's benefactor, William Lancaster

town and at County Hall of concentrating all post-sixteen education in a tertiary college to be based at NORCAT, now The College of West Anglia.

Inevitably there were major changes in the curriculum and organisation of the school at reorganisation. The new first-year intake was divided into two halves, Blue and Yellow, for timetabling purposes. Whereas in the Grammar School teaching had been largely in form groups, streamed by ability, the new groups were setted by ability in different subjects at half term in the first year. The children with the lowest reading scores were separated out and taught in a small group for the core subjects. This pattern was continued until the beginning of the 1990s. Inevitably new courses, such as home economics, were introduced to ensure that the curriculum was appropriate for a mixed and all-ability school.

The pastoral system based on year groups, introduced amidst controversy in the mid-1970s, became much more important in the comprehensive era. In year groups, which might be as big or bigger than the primary schools from which the children had come, it was vital that each student was known as an individual. Their welfare and progress was the primary concern of the Head of Year and his or her team of tutors. One of the chores for tutors over the years would be checking that students were in school uniform. In 1979 the blue blazer was replaced by blue or grey pullovers, although blazers continued to be worn by those who had been admitted to the Grammar School. It was decided at the end of the 1980s to phase out the grey pullovers since many felt that the school did not look to have a proper uniform. One sensible decision made in 1979 was to allow girls to wear trousers or skirts. The only arguments to come over the years would be about the length of their skirts.

Fortunately it had been decided that the comprehensive intakes would be introduced one year at a time. At K.E.S. the first-year mixed and all-ability entry of 234 in 1979 took the school up from

642 pupils in 1978 to 813. By the time of the fifth comprehensive intake in 1983 the roll stood at 1351. The sixth form also grew significantly. It jumped from 109 in 1978 to 149 a year later, although this included only twelve girls. For much of the 1980s the numbers were between 140 and 160 but 1988 saw a significant increase in numbers with 228 sixth formers on the roll in September. This was an important factor in keeping the overall numbers up since the first-year intake had fallen to 168 by 1989. The total roll peaked at 1354 in 1984 and fell thereafter to 1124 in 1989 and 1116 in 1990.

The two years leading up to the change over from a grammar to a comprehensive school were very difficult ones. The Editorial in *The Lennensian* (1979) said that the previous two years must have been among the most eventful and difficult ones since the school was established in its present buildings. The building of a sports hall and craft block, the demolition of the cricket pavilion and the modification of the Head Master's house to provide accommodation for the sixth form meant 'many months working amidst the hurly burly of a construction site – an experience which has put tremendous strain on all concerned, not least the cleaning staff who have battled with a sea of mud sometimes reminiscent of the Somme battlefield.'

Construction of the new Art and Technology block in 1978/79 (D. McCall)

The building programme started in 1978, but, even before it had begun, the plans had to be trimmed back because the tenders, when they came in, were higher than expected. This might have been predicted considering the huge amount of building work needed to complete the county's re-organisation plans. The building of two craft rooms was postponed as was the remodelling of parts of the existing building. However, work did begin on the conversion of what had been the Head Master's house and on the new sports facilities and the main art/craft block. By September 1979 the sports hall and gymnasium were ready for use but it was not until the following January that the craft block, at least in part, was also ready. It was finally completed, along with a separate woodwork room, in time for the summer term. It was not until 1984 that the craft accommodation was as originally planned, with the completion of an additional workshop and another home economics room.

From the beginning of the spring term of 1980 the upper floors of the Head Master's house were in use as a sixth-form centre and the ground floor was used for administration. The Boarding House was converted in stages. During 1980/81 three classrooms were created on the top floor. In addition the *cage room*, by the east door, was made into another classroom. It had been used to store sports equipment (in cages) and boots and shoes, as well as for changing. Some work was also carried out on the boarders' dining room in preparation for its use as a music room once the last boarders had left in the summer of 1982. During 1981/82 a further three classrooms were created on the middle floor of the block and the kitchen was converted into a music room. The annexe at 141 Gaywood Road was sold during 1980 and the boarders were concentrated in the main building.

Restoration work on the pillars of the Ceremonial Gates, damaged by a lorry in 1979

The official re-opening of the restored gateway

Another project underway in 1980 was the improvement in the tennis facilities. The grass courts on the south field were hard surfaced and a year later the hard play area at the north end of the field near the Gaywood Road was converted into four tennis courts with the erection of a 3 metre-high wire fence. Half the cost came from the proceeds of a sponsored run the previous autumn which had raised £1400. The new entrance and drive between the canteen and the tennis courts was also opened in 1981. This had been proposed as early as 1976 by Mr Greaves but the LEA only accepted the need for a new entrance in 1979 after one of the pillars of the ceremonial gates had been damaged by a lorry.

The school's silver cups stolen in October 1980 - a photograph taken in 1934

Other work on the buildings in the early 1980s included the remodelling of science laboratories, the conversion of the Head Master's former study and secretary's office back to a classroom, the removal of wall bars and other equipment from the old gymnasium to allow its use for drama and the installation of a multi-gym in what had been the main cloakroom on the ground floor of the science block. The £3250 insurance money from Norwich Union, following the theft of all the school's trophies in October 1980, was used to pay for the multi-gym. A major improvement came with the purchase of curtains for the hall to help solve the problem of the poor acoustics.

For many Old Lennensians the demolition of Harry's Hut was a sad event. There are many with fond memories of Harry Thornton's mathematics lessons or the preparatory department under George Martin, although perhaps some have less happy memories of the *middle room*, to which miscreants would be sent for the cane in the 1940s. The former sanatorium was taken down in 1982 to make way for the additional craft building and, although it was hoped that it could be re-erected on a new site, this was not to happen. The other features to disappear in the 1980s, which had been part of the school from very early days, were the swimming pool and the cricket pavilion.

1982 also saw the introduction of, to use the words of Prince Charles, 'a great carbuncle' on the face of the school. Thirteen mobile classrooms were sited just to the south of the Boarding House, obscuring one of the best views of the 1906 building. A year later Mr Greaves put forward a strong case for a new classroom block for English and Modern Languages to replace at least some of the mobiles. The proposal was for five classrooms on the ground floor and a new library and resources centre above. Unfortunately it took ten years before such a building was achieved. In fact Mr Greaves was told in no uncertain terms by an officer of the LEA that there was no chance of a major building project for K.E.S. and that if he continued to press for one the school's intake at 11+ would be reduced so that his case for a new building would be undermined. LEAs in the 1980s were all powerful and Mr Greaves clearly believed that the threat would be carried out if he persuaded the governors to press the case. As a result, he reported to governors in March 1984 that it was unlikely the proposal for a new building would come to anything and that 'the best we can hope for is the re-instatement of the minor work to enlarge the existing library.' This was completed and ready to use in the autumn of 1986 but to add insult to injury yet another mobile was needed because one of the two proposed classrooms in the library block had been lost.

Another major change in the character of the school came with the closure of the Boarding House, such an integral part of the school from the earliest days. From fifty full boarders and two day

The south face of the school marred by mobile classrooms in 1986 (Lynn News)

The last boarders – Andrew Walsh and Adrian Clarke, both aged 18, and fifth-former Richard Westwood, in Andrew's study bedroom, June 1982 (EDP)

boarders in 1976/77 the numbers fell gradually once the decision to phase it out had been taken. There were thirty full boarders plus six day boarders in 1978/79 and twelve plus six in 1980/81. It finally closed in July 1982 when the last two sixth formers and one fifth former had taken their examinations.

A major casualty of the early 1980s was *The Lennensian*. It was first published in October 1907 and came out three times a year until the summer of 1957. Inexplicably Edition 151 was followed in 1958 by Volume XX, after which it came out once a year, although Volumes XXXV1 and XXXV11 were published as one and the very last edition covered the two years 1978 and 1979. Due to escalating costs, the decision was taken in October 1981 that the magazine was no longer viable. It had been a marvellous feature of the school. Not only had it offered opportunities for students' work to be published, but it had also provided regular news about staff and student arrivals and departures, successes of various kinds, and details of extra-curricular activities, including sporting fixtures and results. It was very popular with Old Lennensians as a means of keeping in touch with the goings-on in the school, of which the vast majority were very proud. Sadly, because of lack of support, the Old Lennensians' Association too was wound up in the 1980s.

Members of the Norfolk Medieval Association provided entertainment at the 1977 Summer Fete

All in a good cause - Dave Perry suffering the indignity of a drenching also at the 1977 Summer Fete

Another prominent feature of the school had disappeared in the late 1970s – the flagpole. As part of the Queen's Silver Jubilee celebrations in 1977 it was decided to spend £80 on buying a new flag and on repairs to the roping. Unfortunately a gale brought the flagpole down and the decision was taken not to replace it. Yet another link with the past had gone.

On a more positive note, many important changes were made in the late 1970s which brought the school into the modern era. Perhaps the most necessary was the encouragement of parents to become much more actively involved in the school by the formation of a Parent Teacher Association, something Mr Sleigh had resisted. Some 500 parents attended the inaugural meeting in October 1976 at which a constitution was agreed and the first PTA committee elected. Very successful social and fund-raising events were to take place in the following years, such as the PTA Dance in March 1977, attended by over 200, and the Summer Fete in July of the same year. There was also strong financial support from parents for sponsored events aimed at raising money for those items which the LEA would not or could not provide. In the autumn of 1977, for example, over £3200 was raised in a sponsored walk for the purchase of a new mini-bus and a further £900 was contributed from PTA funds. Ten years later a similar event raised £4500 for the same purpose. Perhaps more importantly, the PTA was to be the means through which, on the one hand, the school could consult parents about proposed changes and, on the other, parents could express opinions on issues of concern.

Fund raising for charity had always been a feature of the school and this was to continue. February 1978 saw the first non-uniform day, and this became over the years one of the most popular ways of persuading students to part with their money. The policy of consulting parents was extended to their children in 1980 with the formation of the Charity Committee, a staff-student group which decided each year how money raised for charity should be allocated. Substantial amounts of money were raised each year. In July 1986, for example, Mr Greaves told governors that some £3200 had been raised in the previous six months, including £1441 for Muscular Dystrophy in the annual first-year sponsored swim.

Other innovations which were welcomed by parents included a booking system for parents' evenings introduced in 1977 and an Open Day which was to become an annual event from 1978. A major change for students came in December 1978 when the Annual Prize Giving took place in the evening rather than during the day. It ceased to be compulsory and henceforth was attended only by prize winners and those who had been successful in public examinations and, of course, proud parents.

Developing good relations with what in those days were referred to as feeder primary schools was also seen as important. In part this was to encourage recruitment but more importantly aimed at easing the transition from primary to secondary school. Over the years subject links were established in core subjects such as mathematics and English and events such as the annual link concert and fun sports day, as well as day visits by primary-school pupils, were introduced.

Extra-curricular activities flourished throughout the late 1970s and the 1980s. In 1979 Mr Greaves was able to report on over fifty different activities taking place. A major vehicle for involving large numbers of students remained the house system which saw further changes in 1979 when the eight houses were reduced to four, although the names were all retained: Lancaster/School; Edinburgh/York; Gloucester/Windsor; and Keene/Thoresby. The decision was taken because of the impending closure of the boarding house and comprehensive re-organisation.

One of the great successes of the 1980s was in public speaking. A team, all of whom were at the school from 1977 to 1984, and consisting of James Bolton (Main Speaker), Stephen Morgan (Chairman), and Mark Barker (Vote of Thanks), was placed first in the 1984 English Speaking Union International Public Speaking Final at the American Embassy in Grosvenor Square. The road to the final was a somewhat uneven one. The team was joint winners, with Fakenham High School, in the Norfolk round and went on to the Eastern Regional Finals at Bury St Edmonds where the K.E.S. team won. Then in the National Finals, at the Café Royale in London, K.E.S. came second, although James Bolton was awarded a cup for best speaker. Both the first and second-placed teams then went on to compete against teams from the Commonwealth and Europe in the International Final. James again won the prize as best speaker and the team gained sweet revenge by coming first overall. It is not surprising that from 1985 public speaking was included in the inter-house competition.

Winners of the 1984 ESU International Public Speaking Competition, together with Head of English, Bernard Phillips (EDP)

James Bolton (right) holding the Best Speaker's Cup and Stephen Morgan with the Overall Winner's Cup

On the sporting front it was again in hockey that individual students were successful at national level. In 1979 Ian Oakes (1971-78) and Robin Brundle (1975-80) were chosen, at Senior and U16 levels respectively, as non-travelling reserves for England. Nick Gregory (1973-80), following in the very successful footsteps of his brother Tim, played for the East of England U21 team while still at school and in 1981 was awarded a Hockey Blue at Cambridge. In 1983 a Pelicans seven-a-side team, all K.E.S. students, became successively Norfolk and East Region Champions and runners up in the national final. A year later another Pelicans seven-a-side team, this time with one non-K.E.S. player, won the national title. In 1985 Kevin Smith (1980-87) played for the England U16 team both in the home internationals against Ireland, Scotland and Wales and in a tournament in Brussels involving Belgium, Holland and West

Germany as well as England. Between 1986 and 1988 Danny Kerry (1982-89) played for England at U15, U16 and U18 levels and his brother Sean Kerry (1980-87) was selected for the U21 squad in 1986 and 1987. In 1988 Paul Gyles (1982-89) played in an England Schoolboys' Hockey Xl. Considering its record of success, it seems a great pity that boys' hockey was phased out in 1987 but perhaps this was inevitable following the introduction of rugby in 1982-83 and the retirement of Ken Gregory, the chief hockey coach, in 1986. However a legacy of this period in the school's history is the highly successful career of Danny Kerry.

In August 2018 Danny Kerry MBE was appointed Head Coach of the Great Britain and England men's hockey teams after some eleven years as Head Coach of the women's international teams. According to the official GB Hockey website, 'Danny is the most successful coach in British hockey history, having led the England and Great Britain's women to numerous successes' including a magnificent Gold Medal at the Rio Games in 2016.

The photograph shows the school's rugby team in January 1983 shortly before their first competitive match on the new rugby pitch at K.E.S. The team, which beat Thetford Grammar School by 16 points to 6, included twelve present and three former students and was captained by England Colts triallist, Mark Smith.

The school rugby team in January 1983 shortly before beating Thetford Grammar School by 16 points to 6

Cricket continued to thrive despite the problem of finding other state schools against which to compete. In 1984 K.E.S. was the only LEA school in Norfolk able to field six teams on a Saturday and an increasing number of matches was played against independent schools such as Gresham's at Holt. One of the cricketing stars of the 1980s was Rodney Bunting (1982-87) who went on to play for Northamptonshire and later for Sussex.

Sport was not however just for an elite. Participation of students of all abilities was encouraged and there were house and school teams in a wide range of winter and summer sports supported by keen and enthusiastic staff, and not just those who were members of the PE Department. Even tchouk ball flourished for a few years.

In Mr Greaves' time, as well as in that of his predecessor, school drama went through periods of relative inactivity. Both musical and straight plays were produced in the early 1980s *including Beowulf, All the King's Men, Peter Grimes, The Threepenny Opera, The Tinker's Wedding, A Den of Thieves, A Christmas Carol,* and *Sherlock Holmes* but when *Macbeth* was put on in March 1986 it was described as the most ambitious dramatic venture for some time. With a highly acclaimed production of *The Importance of Being Earnest* in November of the same year, drama was seen as having come of age.

Music, like drama, was at a low ebb in the middle of the 1970s and soon after his arrival Mr Greaves showed a determination to do something about it. A concert held in May 1977 was said to be the first for at least twenty years. He firmly believed that the school should have an orchestra and he realised that if this was to come about there would have to be both some musical instruments available for loan and also tuition in playing them provided. He told governors early in 1977 that the times were 'unfortunately most unpropitious for the rapid development which I see necessary here.' The LEA peripatetic teachers' time was already fully used elsewhere and there was no money available for musical instruments. The governors agreed to provide £200 for the purchase of musical instruments and from September a small amount of tuition was provided by the LEA. Two hours per week for strings and one and a half hours for woodwind were hardly adequate amounts of teaching time, but it was a start, and more time would be provided in future years. At Speech Day in 1981 Mr Greaves was able to announce that music was 'entering a period of renewed growth....We have built up to one concert every term, together with other established musical occasions such as the Carol Service.' By the end of 1985 he proudly commented on the transformation that had taken place in music in the past six years, as demonstrated by the fact that there had been two concerts in December 1984 and two more in the summer term of 1985, the last under David Steele who left at the end of that term.

Mr Greaves's interest in developing music was also demonstrated by his support for the formation of the West Norfolk Jubilee Youth Orchestra in 1977. The idea had been proposed by Richard Griffiths, who became the first chairman of the orchestra committee. In 1980, Mr Greaves also supported the establishment of the West Norfolk Music Centre, at first based in the old Girls' High School buildings at King Street but later transferred to the Queensway site of Springwood High School. When he commended it to parents at Speech Day the same year one hundred children of all ages were already taking advantage of the opportunity for tuition in both instrumental and choral music and he described it as an 'outstanding success.'

By the end of the 1980s, as well as theatre trips and field courses, many foreign trips were available to K.E.S. students. The first of many ski trips, to Switzerland in 1980, was led by Paul Tebay, and he was also to organise very successful sporting tours both within this country and abroad, such as that to Switzerland in the 1982 Easter holidays. Building on the success of the French exchange a second one was organised to Avila in Spain in 1986, the twenty-fifth anniversary of the link with Brive. Another very popular trip which was started in the late 1980s was the annual water sports holiday to Anduze in southern France and there were trips to Dieppe and to Boulogne.

A number of long-serving staff left in the late 1970s and 1980s. One of the first to go was Harry

Thornton. He retired in 1980 from his post as Head of the Mathematics Department which, according to Mr Greaves, 'he was able to hand over as a highly successful going concern. This owed much to the fact that although he was nearing the end of his career, (he) always kept his mind open to the possibility of worthwhile innovation, while maintaining an extremely healthy scepticism in avoiding the temptations of band-wagon jumping.' Mike Boagey (1959-66) says that Harry Thornton was a 'great guy.' He 'used to ask us to calculate the probability of having six daughters… Needless to say Harry had six daughters. I owe this guy my whole career.' Tim Carney (1974-81) remembers that he 'gave a great speech on his retirement - can't remember all of it but I do remember it went down well with the pupils – not so well with the Head!'

Doug McCall, on the staff from 1955, is a man of whom Kevin Ellen (1976-83) has some fond memories.

'Not only a master of his craft but also a man who bonded with boys, never seemed to have trouble and worked furiously behind his bench as the line of boys with problems with their jobs lined up in front of him…The guy was a hero and a true friend….Despite putting a saw half way through my thumb in the first year, woodwork remained one of my favourite subjects and still is a favourite hobby.'

For Steve Tuck (1975-82) too he was 'truly special,' and he recalled: 'He made my snooker cue case which still carries my cue to this day.' When Mr McCall officially retired in 1981, Mr Greaves paid fulsome tribute, telling governors that 'no colleague has contributed more to the school, over very many years, than Doug….He will be sorely missed, for his friendliness, for his understanding of his students and for the example he sets to us all.' In the event Doug McCall returned to teach part time for a further two years before he finally retired.

In 1983 Dave Perry retired after 30 years at the school. According to Mr Greaves he was 'notorious for a certain inability to read the lower figures on the old swimming pool thermometer' and 'he had an equally robust approach to his pupils in other aspects of physical education.' However recalling visits from many Old Lennensians over the years who had asked about Mr Perry, he continued: 'If it is true that some of them tremble a bit at the memory of those days, it is also very obvious how real was the affection with which he is remembered.' Certainly, as in earlier years, a PE lesson involving swimming was not very popular, as Steve Tuck recalls:

'I can see it now, a grim line of skinny, greyish-white, shivering twelve year olds standing along the length of the pool, shortest to tallest. Then in full view of everyone….(Mr Perry) dipped his bare elbow into the water for one nano-second and proclaimed it 'up to temperature'….What followed defied logic. Thirty boys seemingly appeared as if by magic on the opposite side of the pool…..The one testament to them having actually touched the water was the foaming turmoil they left behind.'

Any readers who are or have been teachers will feel considerable sympathy for the situation Dave Perry found himself in as a result of a practical joke played by Brian Krill (1950-55) on the sports field one summer:

'I picked up a javelin, tucked it under my left armpit, held it in place with my right hand on my chest, let out a yell and staggered onto the field. I then collapsed to my knees, then full length and remained motionless. Now I always knew that Dave Perry was a pretty fit sort of chap but the speed at which he reached my side truly amazed me….I did not say a word but just stared up at him and slowly winked. Dave Perry's pallor changed from magnolia to what I can now best describe as an exquisite shade of claret. Three detentions later I was still, wondering whether the jape was worth it.'

One of the best-remembered teachers who retired in this period was Ken Gregory who was at the school for 34 years from 1952. At Speech Day in 1986 Mr Greaves said that 'many generations of pupils benefited from his enthusiasm, skills and gifts of teaching. No one can doubt that the greatest of these was, in my day at least, hockey.' However, it was his skill as a teacher of English which was appreciated by Martin Twist (1976-80), now known as Martin Sterling:

'I owe this man my career – my life, in fact. He stirred possibilities in me that had hitherto only been dreams. He was the first to take my writing seriously. I don't know if he ever believed back then I could actually make a living from words. But I'm glad I wrote to him once and told him that I could, and that I was. He was also a damned good teacher. The best.'

Robin Sainty (1968-75) agrees:

'Along with Japes [J P Smallwood] the greatest I've ever met and one of the nicest people. I had the privilege of visiting him a couple of times shortly before his tragic death from cancer and even in severe ill health he was a model of courtesy and genuinely keen for any gossip about the school and the pupils that he remembered. A truly sad loss.'

And from Mark Buxton, (1967-74): 'What an inspiration to all us young lads. Football, hockey and cricket were his passion; and he was a pretty damn good English teacher too.' David Cobbold (1945-53) remembers him coming to the school. He saw him as radical, modern and informal and someone who believed that learning should be fun, discipline light and boys put on trust, in contrast to the prevailing ethos in the school at that time. A few months after Ken Gregory's death in 1997 a special cricket match was staged at school in his memory. Nine members of the 1975 *Oval Boys*, together with Tim and Nick Gregory, played against the School 1st XI. The visitors lost by a single run but for all of them it was a memorable occasion.

Other long-serving staff who retired in this period included Ronald Fisk in 1977, David Whitmarsh-Knight in 1978, Aubrey Hood in 1979, Peter Sykes in 1984, Bryan Seaman in 1985 and Alan Middleton also in 1985.

A most difficult period in the 1980s for K.E.S., and indeed for most schools in the state sector, resulted from the industrial action called by the teacher unions which were in conflict with the Government over pay and working conditions. For much of 1985 and 1986 members of two particular teachers' unions were working to rule. In effect this meant that many of them would not teach classes over thirty, would not run extra-curricular activities and would not do lunch- time duties. Even those teachers who were not involved were instructed by their unions not to cover for colleagues who were working to rule. The extra-curricular programme at K.E.S. was not hit as badly as in many other schools but sport, in particular, was severely curtailed, if only because other teams were not available to play on Saturdays. Despite the problems, Mr Greaves was able to report that in the school year 1984/85, taking all sports together, there had been 468 inter-school matches and an even greater number of house fixtures.

The refusal of teachers to supervise students at lunchtime was a major problem as it left only the Head Master and the deputies to do the duties. For health and safety reasons, as at many other schools, it was decided that all but the youngest children had to be sent off the site at lunchtimes because otherwise there were too many to supervise safely. This was very unpopular with the parents and the local community, but until a deal was struck with the Government in the summer of 1986, by which midday supervisors would be paid, the pressures on the senior staff in schools were considerable.

Largely as a solution to the problem of mid-day supervision, Mr Greaves proposed a radical change in the pattern of the school day, which is still, with some modifications, in place today. In its original form the proposal put to the governors was for school to start at 8.10 am and to finish at 2.35 pm with a twenty-minute break in the morning and just thirty minutes for lunch. After extensive consultation with staff and parents, it was decided to change to an 8.40 am start and a 2.40 pm finish. Some governors wanted another half an hour at the end of the day but the Head Master argued that this was not acceptable to staff who, worried about fatigue, would only agree to the very short lunch break if there was an early finish in the afternoon. There were many advantages put forward for the early finish, not least the time that would then be available for extra-curricular activities or homework for the children, and time for meetings, marking and preparation for staff.

It was decided to try out the new format for the school day during the second half of the summer term 1987 and to review the effects of the change at the summer meeting of governors. However at that meeting it was realised that the experiment had not been running long enough to make an informed judgement and so it was decided to extend the trial to Easter 1988. By then the vast majority of parents were happy that the new times should be retained. Although other schools in the county did not take up the semi-continental day pioneered by K.E.S., it was generally accepted as a great success. In neither of the Ofsted Inspections in 1995 and 2000 was it suggested that the shorter day had had a negative effect on examination results.

How successful was the school in academic terms under Mr Greaves? There was no full HMI inspection during his headship. In fact there was not one between that in 1957 under Mr Sleigh and the first OFSTED inspection in 1995 during my time as Head. Towards the end of November 1985 a group of six HMI visited the school and looked at a number of departments. They discussed their findings, which 'were in the main favourable', with the Head Master but no formal report was published. The Modern Languages Department was inspected in 1988 and was reported to be 'outstanding in the development of modern technology and in the success of its use of new methods.' To get an idea of overall standards we must therefore analyse examinations results in some detail.

From 1976 to 1984 the examination classes consisted, for the most part, of students admitted when it was a grammar school. One would expect the results therefore to be very similar to those in the first half of the 1970s. To some extent they were, although there were the normal fluctuations that schools find because each cohort of students varies not only in terms of ability but also in attitude and motivation. At 'A' level the pass rate stayed at 78% for the three years 1977 to 1979 and reached that figure again in 1983. However for most of the other years in the 1980s results were lower, falling to 64% in 1982 and 65% in 1988. However Mr Greaves left on a high point in 'A' level terms because the 1989 pass rate was a record 80% and came from the biggest-ever entry of 89 students. The percentage of students gaining A grades, at 9.5, was only about half the highest figures achieved – 17.6% in 1979 and 17% in 1983, although the actual number of As was higher than in 1979. Nevertheless Mr Greaves rightly reported the 'A' level results to the governors 'with immense pride and pleasure.'

At 'O' level the highest percentage figure for students gaining five or more passes peaked in 1977 at 84%, although it was a small cohort of 58 students. The equivalent percentage figures for the years 1979 to 1981 were lower, although the actual number of pupils achieving five or more 'O' levels in each year rose to over 70 compared with only 40 in 1977. From 1982 however both the numbers and the percentages fell markedly. The low points were in 1985 and 1986, when only 42 and 44 students gained five or more 'O' level passes, representing 37.8% and 35.7% of the cohorts respectively. These were the second and third fully comprehensive intakes. At this time students were able to take either or both GCE 'O' levels or CSEs and it is likely that staff were giving as many students as possible the chance to take the more highly-regarded examination; hence the low percentage figures. Perhaps they were over ambitious.

It was inevitable that the number of students capable of gaining 'O' levels would fall. The boys who had formerly made up the grammar school intake had come from all over West Norfolk, and indeed far beyond to join the Boarding House. Under the new comprehensive system, although K.E.S. was now admitting girls who would previously have gone to The King's Lynn High School, it had lost able boys, not only to the other two Lynn secondary schools, but also to those at Terrington St Clement, Marshland and Hunstanton. Furthermore some parents, whose children would in the past have gained places at the Grammar School or the Girls' High School, were dissatisfied with the new comprehensive system, and were deciding to pay for private education.

1988 was the year in which the GCSE examination replaced GCE 'O' level and the CSE. For the first time all the students in the school sat the same examination and were graded on a pass scale from A to G, with the top three grades equivalent to the old 'O' level pass. The results would act as a baseline for those in the future. Out of a year group of 211 students, 79 (or 37%) gained at least five higher grades. The actual number matched the best results of the early 1980s, although from a cohort which was twice the size. The number gaining five or more higher grades did fall to 59 (or 32%) the following year, but Mr Greaves pointed out to the governors that this was not as strong a year academically as the previous one.

K.E.S. students from the 1970s and 1980s have been successful in a wide range of professions and occupations. For example, James Bolton (1977-84) is a consultant psychiatrist at St Helier Hospital in London, an Honorary Senior Lecturer at St George's University of London and Chair of the Faculty of Liaison Psychiatry at the Royal College of Psychiatrists; Claire Williams (1982 to 1989), is Associate Professor of Brazilian Literature and Culture in the University of Oxford and a Fellow of St Peter's College; and Matthew Shaw (1983-1990), who has worked for the BBC since 2006, was appointed UK Futures Editor for BBC News in 2017.

One of Mr Greaves's greatest achievements was to leave the school with what in 1989 was state of the art equipment in Information Technology. At the 1987 Speech Day he announced the launch of an IT Campaign with the aim of raising £73,400 for new computers. The fund was given a kick start by a most generous donation of £5000 from Bespak. This was arranged by Andrew Schumann, then a governor of the school as well as a Director of Bespak, in memory of his father, Alex, the company's founder. Two of the Cambridge colleges with which K.E.S. had long links had also promised to support the campaign: Trinity had promised £2000; and St John's College £1000. A growing list of local companies contributed, as did some grant-making trusts. With a £5000 donation, one of the most generous was the Garfield Weston Foundation which had links with Anglia Canners. The school and the PTA were themselves very active in fund raising and Mr Greaves at Speech Day in December 1988 announced: 'There has never been a period when everyone, adult and child alike, has worked so hard for an additional common purpose for so long a period.' One of the highlights was the official public launch of the campaign in a three-hour Radio Norfolk broadcast by Roy Waller from the school in May of 1988.

Although the original target was not met, some £42,000 was raised by the spring of 1989, and this was enough to fit out a computer room. In addition another company was to more than make up for the shortfall by offering to furnish and equip a further room. K.E.S. became one of a small number of flagship schools for ICL and C12 (on the top floor of what had been the boarding wing) was to provide an excellent facility for a new sixth-form course, the B TEC Diploma in Business Studies. The computer equipment was leased to the school at a cost which was originally well below the market rate. This new room was officially opened on 21 April 1989 by Lord Keith, then the Chairman of STC, ICL's parent company.

The main effects of the 1988 Education Act, which brought in the National Curriculum, Local Management of Schools, Open Enrolment and Grant Maintained Schools, were not to be seen until the 1990s. However, in March 1989 Mr Greaves made a strong case to the governors for becoming Grant Maintained. He felt that the school had been badly neglected by the LEA both in the 1970s, as a result of what he referred to as 'planning blight' caused by uncertainties on comprehensive re-organisation, and in more recent years. His request in 1983 for a new classroom block for English and Modern Languages, to replace mobiles, had been rejected and there had been a long-running battle to get increased resources and adequate numbers of non-teaching staff. Mr Greaves argued that if the school became Grant Maintained there would not only be significant financial advantages, but governors would have control of admission arrangements as well as suspensions and exclusions. He believed that there was at least a chance that the Department for Education and Science would be more sympathetic to the request for new buildings than the LEA. He also felt that if the school became Grant Maintained the Sixth Form would be safe from any attempts by the LEA to introduce changes in the pattern of post-16 education in King's Lynn.

The K.E.S. Governors held two Special Meetings on 25 April 1989 to consider opting out of LEA control. At the first they heard a presentation from a representative of the Grant Maintained Trust and one from Michael Edwards, the County Education Officer. Later in the day they discussed the pros and cons and in the end decided by 11 votes to 7, with one abstention, that they would not at that stage ballot parents on the issue of going Grant Maintained. Perhaps the fact that Mr Greaves was to retire at Christmas and would not be leading the school if it became Grant Maintained affected how some people voted. The CEO's indication that K.E.S. was likely to gain financially under Local Management and his declared willingness to look again at the question of new buildings may also have influenced the voting.

For Mr Greaves, opting out of LEA control would have given the school a 'fresh start' and 'the opportunity to recapture lost ground.' This last statement was a clear acknowledgement that the reputation of the school had suffered in recent years. The first-year intake in September 1989 was only 168, despite work by the school's Image Committee and visits by staff to partner primary schools to speak to parents. Inevitably the change from a grammar school to a comprehensive had been difficult for some staff who had not been able to adjust to teaching children of all abilities. The perception of the local community was that discipline and behaviour were not what they had been and results no longer seemed to be as good. The independent sector and the other two high schools in the town were, for various reasons, attracting children from the traditional catchment area, although there was also a movement from the other areas of the town to K.E.S.

With the introduction of Open Enrolment, which gave parents the right to request a place for their children at a particular secondary school, rather than be allocated a place depending on their postal address, the Heads of the three Lynn high schools came to an agreement, in July 1989, aimed at avoiding open competition. They adopted a number of measures to achieve this goal: prospectuses would only be sent to parents either living in the traditional catchment area of a school or whose children attended a partner primary school; similarly only those same parents would receive specific invitations to visit a high school, although Open Days would be advertised in the press and be open to anyone; and high school staff would only make personal presentations to parents of partner primary schools, even if invited to do otherwise. In a report to the governors, Mr Greaves said that there had been clear attempts to attract children in one of the K.E.S. partner schools to another high school. Rather than retaliating in like manner he had proposed the agreement.

How does Mr Greaves assess what was achieved during his time as Head Master?

'My overriding ambition since before reorganisation had been and remained to retain in the 'new' school all the best of the old: its academic and sporting standards; its pre-eminence in the town and in the county; its sense of its own history. I aimed to develop in the comprehensive school a strong belief in service to the community and in the wider world. And I proposed to create within the school community a greater sense of responsibility and mutual respect. I am sure that the successful integration of the female of the species into the community contributed immeasurably to those ambitions.'

However he remembers his time at K.E.S.

'as a period of constant battles to make inadequate resources go as far as possible to meeting our pupils' needs. That we achieved so much of what I had hoped for at KES is down to the selfless determination of all our staff. How much more could have been done with reasonable financial provision was left to my successors to prove and their success has given me enormous pride and satisfaction. I do like to feel that we laid firm foundations for the future.'

Mr Greaves retired in December 1989 and during the Spring Term of 1990, before I took up my appointment in April, Richard Griffiths was Acting Head for the second time. He had also been in charge in the Spring Term of 1985 when Mr Greaves had a sabbatical at Cambridge and he was also to stand in for me, for a similar reason, in the summer term of 1996. On each occasion he did a wonderful job.

My arrival coincided with the introduction of local management of schools, the most successful of the changes brought in by the 1988 Education Act. For the first time schools would have control over the bulk of their budgets and would be free to use money in the best interests of the students. A new era was about to begin.

7. Into the Twenty-first Century

Like Dick Greaves, my background was in the state sector. I had been a deputy head in a mixed comprehensive in Oxfordshire for six years and then, for eight years, Head of Buxton College, a boys' comprehensive school in Derbyshire. My time as Head from 1990 to 2002 was challenging but very enjoyable, not least because my arrival, in April 1990, coincided with a most exciting change, the introduction of Local Management of Schools (LMS). For the first time schools were to receive the bulk of the money allocated by the Government for the education of children. LEAs were allowed to keep back funding for school transport, special educational needs and support services but money to cover staff salaries and premises costs, as well as books and equipment, was to be delegated. Up to that point, schools had only received from the LEAs money to cover teaching materials such as paper, exercise books, textbooks and equipment, in the case of K.E.S. a figure of £52,623 in 1989/90. In contrast the school's budget for the following financial year was £1.7 million. By 2001/02 the figure had doubled to around £3.5 million, partly because of increases due to inflation and further delegation of funding but also because the school was much bigger. Under LMS there was not only a much larger amount of money within the control of the school but also, within certain limits, it could use the money as it saw fit. For K.E.S this proved to be very beneficial. Considerable improvements to the fabric of the building were achieved to remedy the neglect by the LEA in the 1980s and before. In addition a new classroom block was built to replace twelve of the mobiles brought on site in the early 1980s and this was only possible because the school made a substantial contribution towards the cost.

What was the school like towards the end of the twentieth century? Would it be easily recognised by those from previous eras? The hall with its barrel roof, surmounted by the lantern tower, is still the most striking internal feature of the school; visitors always express their surprise and admiration. It is very impressive. Careful scrutiny of the hall tells a great deal about the school's history. The portraits in oils by local artist Fred Roe of Henry Vlll and Edward Vll indicate the dates of the original foundation and of the new building, as do the statues of the Tudor and Edwardian scholars, mounted in alcoves on either side of the clock on the outside of the building. The Gold Medal Board, the War Memorials, the Honours Boards, the clock with its gold-leafed motto, *Crescat in horas doctrina* (*Let him hourly increase in learning*), and the bronze plaque under the portrait of Sir William Lancaster all play their part in telling the history of the school.

In addition to the 1906 building, with its three different blocks of two and three storeys, linked by corridors and courtyards, there is the building opened by the Queen in 1956 on the back drive, the library dating from 1969 and modified in 1986, the Art and Technology block built in the early 1980s when the school became comprehensive, the sports centre opened in 1991, albeit replacing that built in 1979, and the twelve-classroom block opened in January 1994. This reduced the number of mobile classrooms from fourteen but there were still six mobiles, two of them fitted out as science laboratories.

Tragically the statue of the Tudor scholar was stolen in March 1993. Thieves climbed up onto the roof one weekend and prised the statue off its plinth. Whether it was stolen for the metal content or as a statue is not known but it was never recovered. If the thieves thought that the statue was bronze they must have been disappointed as it was only bronze coating on a concrete body. This was discovered when the Edwardian scholar, which had been loosened but not removed, was taken down for safe keeping. Plaster-cast replicas were made and placed outside in the alcoves and since

A dark day for the Head: the theft of the Tudor statue in 1993 (Lynn News)

The Edwardian Statue removed to the entrance lobby

February 1995 the original Edwardian statue has stood on a specially made wooden plinth in the entrance lobby to the school hall.

In the 1990s two excellent new facilities were built. The first was made necessary because of a fire in April 1990 which completely destroyed the sports hall and gymnasium, built in 1979 at the time of comprehensive re-organisation. Since there had not been enough storage space in the building, the PTA had paid for a wooden shed to be erected, at the side, in which PE mats and other equipment were stored. It was a false economy by the LEA which had built a sports facility with inadequate storage. One Sunday afternoon some teenagers from the local area (but not students from K.E.S.) caused a disastrous fire by flicking lighted cigarette ends into the shed. The fire took hold very quickly and spread to the main building. I returned from a weekend visit to my family in Buxton to find the school on the local television news. It was one week after I had taken up my appointment. When I saw the building the next day it looked like a failed soufflé, with the whole of the roof collapsed inwards. For a year and a half the school was without indoor facilities, which made it a difficult time for both staff and students. However, the LEA was very helpful and provided money for additional staffing, transport and for the hire of facilities at the recently opened Lynn Sport.

The new sporting facility, which rose from the ashes, cost some £650,000 and was of a much higher standard than the one it replaced. The sports hall was marked out for badminton, basketball, five-a-side soccer, netball, tennis and volleyball and there were also indoor cricket nets. In addition the new gymnasium had a sprung floor and was fitted out with high-standard equipment. A viewing gallery looking down into the sports hall and gymnasium made it possible to view matches or observe coaching. Unlike the old facility, there was also an outside balcony with excellent views of the pitches and running track.

The Queen's representative on the governing body, Canon George Hall, Rector of Sandringham, was very helpful in arranging for a member of the Royal Family to come to open the new sports centre in November 1991. The Duke of York spent an hour and a quarter at the school. He was shown the school hall and told a little of the school history before being escorted to the sports centre, where he unveiled a commemorative plaque, which was later fixed in the entrance corridor. He then toured the new facility, expressing considerable interest in what he saw, talking

The 1979 sports hall on fire in April 1990 (Lynn News)

The interior of the sports hall completely gutted (Lynn News)

The remnants of the 1979 sports hall (Lynn News)

to and joking with staff and students. Prince Andrew also paid a brief visit to Art, CDT and English classrooms, although by the time he reached the latter the bell had already gone and the low-ability Year 10 group were definitely not keen on a long stay! The Duke rounded off his visit by chatting informally to representatives of the governors, staff, students and parents who had been invited for refreshments in the library. He signed an official photograph and was presented with a K.E.S. sweatshirt. Whether he ever wore it is unknown.

Responding to some prompting the Duke challenged the representatives of the LEA to produce the money needed for a new building to replace the school's fourteen mobile classrooms. It may have helped since it was eventually agreed that the new building would be completed in one phase rather than the proposed two stages. There had been a campaign to get a major building project for some time and the replacement of twelve of the mobiles by a new teaching block in 1993/94 was a major achievement. The new classroom block was opened, in January 1994, by William Kerkham, Chairman of Governors (1988-93), whose dogged pursuit of the County Education Officer, Michael Edwards, had contributed in no small measure to a most satisfactory result for the School. On the ground floor are six classroom for English and on the first floor a further six classrooms for modern languages. These had been the two departments based largely in mobiles, and so the move to a modern and attractive teaching block, with carpeted floors and curtained windows, was warmly welcomed by the staff and pupils.

The official opening of the new teaching block. (From left to right: William Kerkham, Michael Edwards, Brigitte Hamilton (Head of Modern Languages), Mary Tebay (Head of English), the Mayor, Councillor Charles Matkin and Michael Walker (Lynn News)

The saga of this building, called D Block, had been a long-running one. Even after the school had persuaded the LEA of the need to get rid of as many of the mobiles as possible and a building project was agreed, the school was faced with the prospect of it being put up in two phases because of the cost, over £600,000. The governors started by offering £20,000 towards the cost to try to ensure that it was built in one phase. They pointed out all the extra costs involved in a two-phase scheme. Eventually the school ended up paying roughly one third of the total cost but had achieved an excellent new teaching block, similar in some respects to that first suggested by Mr Greaves in 1985. Unfortunately, the rooms on the first floor proved to be much too hot in summer. The County Architect accepted responsibility for the faulty design and agreed to fit air-conditioning units in the first-floor classrooms. This work was not completed until the Autumn Term of 1997.

Earlier, there had been problems about the design. The Planning Committee of the Borough Council had turned it down on the grounds that it did not fit in with the 1906 building. School staff had little sympathy with that view since, apart from the discomfort of working in them, the fourteen mobiles were a far greater blot on the landscape than the proposed building could ever be. Fortunately the County Council Planning Committee, which had the final say, overturned the Borough Council decision.

Even after the completion of the new classroom block there were still five mobiles, including one for science. An additional mobile science laboratory was provided in February 1995. So the school continued to press the LEA for a further building programme but without success. The Education Officer responsible for capital projects agreed, in the autumn of 1998, that feasibility studies would be carried out to see what might be included in the building programme. Nothing came of this except that in 2000 one of the County Architects drew up a plan to put a mezzanine floor in the old gymnasium so as to create badly needed additional accommodation for science. Unfortunately, the scheme would only have resulted in one additional laboratory and a smaller room that could have been used for ICT. At a projected cost of over £200,000 it was decided that other solutions had to be found to solve the problem. Interestingly, back in 1964 when the school was looking at ways of increasing accommodation, one proposal was to build a new gymnasium and use the old one for a library. It was also proposed that it should be divided horizontally to provide additional accommodation.

In addition to the new buildings, improvements were made to the existing fabric in the 1990s. Almost all the classroom floors were carpeted, thus greatly reducing the noise that had previously accompanied any movement of chairs and tables. One result was that it had a calming effect on the pupils' behaviour. A major programme of decoration and refurbishment was also implemented. Many small changes were made to provide better teaching and office space, one of the most successful being the conversion of the old gymnasium into a drama studio. The ceiling was lowered and the floor carpeted to make an excellent facility for drama which subsequently became a popular and successful GCSE option.

One of the exterior improvements completed was the erection of palisade fencing round the perimeter of the school, except along the Gaywood Road, where new railings and new gates were installed in 1998. The total cost was over £60,000, towards which the LEA paid £30,000 from funds available for improvements in school security. Additionally the school was fortunate to gain a grant of £20,000 from the Borough Council's Visual Image Fund towards the cost of the railings and gates, which came to over £42,000. To match the Memorial Gates the new ones were designed with the monogram ER, which can be taken to represent either Elizabeth Regina or Edward Rex.

This work followed major security problems during 1996/97 when, among other measures, the entry to the school from King George V Avenue was bricked up.

A major change in the status of the school came in September 2000 when it became a specialist sports college and, as a result, benefited from substantial additional government funding. A capital grant of £100,000, which had to be matched by a similar amount from sponsorship, was used to upgrade the school's tennis facilities. The old cadet hut, which by the end of the 1980s was being used to store PE equipment and sailing dinghies, was dramatically transformed in 2001 when some £150,000 was spent on its conversion to a tennis club house, with changing facilities, a viewing area and kitchenette. At the same time the tennis courts by the main road were re-laid and floodlit at a cost of about £100,000. The school was fortunate to receive a very good level of support from many local businesses. Particularly generous sponsorship was received from Middleton Aggregates, owned by David (1972-79) and Peter Lemon (1974-81) and from Brundle Motors, as well as from several sports bodies, the PTA and from Trinity and Emmanuel Colleges at Cambridge. A special grant of £50,000 was also received from the Lawn Tennis Association which had designated the school as an LTA tennis development centre.

In addition to the capital grant of £100,000, there was an annual grant of over £135,000, for four years in the first instance. At least £40,000 had to be spent on achieving targets related to the community development plan as opposed to the school curriculum plan. The following year K.E.S was asked to be the principal school in a further development, the Sports Co-ordinator Programme, aimed at spreading good practice in sport to the partner primary schools of other secondary schools in King's Lynn and those at Terrington St Clement and Marshland. This was later expanded to include even more areas. It must be stressed that the overall school curriculum offered by the school was in no way limited by the new sports focus. It was a win-win situation.

Extra-curricular activities were a strong feature of K.E.S. in the 1980s and this aspect of school life was continued and strengthened in the 1990s, a fact which was recognised in both OFSTED reports:

> 'The school provides an exceptionally wide range of extra-curricular activities and many teachers give unstintingly of their own time to support this work.' (OFSTED, 1995.)

> 'An excellent and full programme of extra-curricular activities complements and enriches pupils' learning experiences and their attainment in the formal curriculum.' (OFSTED, 2000.)

The inter-house competition was still a major feature of the extra-curricular life of the school, but the fight for the Dornay Cup, donated by a local firm in the 1980s, was no longer restricted to sporting competitions and included a range of other activities such as public speaking, art, music and science. In all over twenty different competitions contributed to the overall totals. The original Inter-House Challenge Shield which was presented to the school by the Tuck Shop in 1910 had become the Football Shield.

In sport, soccer, rugby, cricket, hockey, netball, tennis, athletics and cross-country involved very large numbers of students each year, in house teams or school teams or both. Every year students were selected to represent West Norfolk, Norfolk or the Eastern Counties and often, as in previous decades, some reached the finals of national competitions. The school has been particularly successful in both athletics and cross-country running. In 1995/96, for example, Hayley Smith (1993-98) was a finalist in the English Schools' Athletics Championships. In 1996/97 Jodie Palmer (1995-2000) was 5th in the National Cross-Country Championships and Chris Hodson (1992-99) was 5th in the English Schools' Multi-event Championships. The following year Jodie was placed 1st in the Intermediate Girls' race in the London Mini-Marathon Inter-City Challenge and Chris was awarded the Sir George Kenny Trophy for 'the most outstanding track athlete of the year' in Norfolk. In 1998/99 he was a finalist in the Senior Boys 110 m hurdles in the English Schools' Athletic Championships. The school's success in the London Mini-Marathon was even greater in 1999 when both the Junior and Intermediate Girls' teams took 1st place and Elizabeth Gerrard won the under-14 race. Although not a city school, K.E.S. took part in the Mini Marathon as the Norwich representative, because none of the schools in the city accepted the challenge to take part!

Two of the school's most successful athletes in the early 2000s were Charlie Waite and Gillian Moss. Charlie, in Year 9, came 2nd in the National Schools' Biathlon Championships in Sheffield in 2002. Although he finished equal first on points, he was awarded second place because he came second in swimming which took precedence over the running race which he won. Gillian, in Year 9, became the 2003 English under-15 Girls' No 1 over 800 metres, having won all three national titles, the Amateur Athletic Association Indoor and Outdoor titles and the All-England Schools' title. She was named Girls' under-15 Athlete of the Year by the Norfolk Amateur Athletic Association.

Several boys were offered professional contracts with football clubs in the 1990s. In cricket the outstanding player of the decade was Robert Ferley (1993-98) who between 1997 and 2000 played for England at under-15, under-16 and under-19 levels. Another outstanding sportsman of the 1990s was Adam Brewer (1991-98) who was 3rd in the Junior Boys' English Table Tennis Championships in 1995/96 and two years later, in the British Schools Tournament in Scotland, brought back a gold medal as part of the winning English team and two silver medals from his singles and doubles matches. K.E.S. students were also very successful in sports for which there are no school teams, for example, in 2002 Helen Brown (1997-2004) was selected for the England Ladies' Volleyball squad and Lauren Ely (1998-2005) played in the England Junior Women's Basketball team.

Not only did the school have some outstanding individual and team successes but it's excellent contribution to the development of sport both in school and in the local community has been recognised in a number of ways. In March 2001 K.E.S was awarded the FA Chartermark and in December the Sport England Gold Sports Mark. The latter replaced the Sports Mark held by the school since 1997. This was also the year in which the school was chosen as a Tennis Development Centre by the Lawn Tennis Association and it is not surprising therefore that the capital project, which formed part of the Sports College bid, was to improve tennis facilities for use by the school and the community.

For the past thirty years or so the Duke of Edinburgh Award scheme has provided opportunities for students to develop character skills and participate in outdoor activities. The scheme has waxed and waned depending on staff interest and expertise but certainly in recent years many students have benefited from the chance to take part. Newer schemes such as the Community Sports Leaders' and Junior Sports Leaders' Awards and Millennium Volunteers, introduced in the 1990s, have also proved excellent both in terms of character-building and community involvement. Having been very successful on both the CSLA and Millennium Volunteers programmes, Gemma Godfrey (1994-2001) won the 2001 Sport England Mick Bradley Award for 'the young person who has made the most significant contribution to sport' in the Eastern Region. Four other CSLA students who attended a week-long camp at Loughborough University in the summer of 2001 won the best-team award and their prize was to have been an all-expenses paid trip to Hampden Academy in Maine in October. Because of the twin towers tragedy on September 11th in New York the trip was postponed. However the very popular alternative prize was a trip to the Winter Olympics at Salt Lake City in March 2002, accompanying the British Team. Shortly after his return to England, one of the four students, Tim Calloway (1998-2002), was invited to report on the trip at the opening of the Sports Colleges Annual Conference at Nottingham University and he proved to be an excellent ambassador for the school.

Compared with some earlier periods in the school's history, drama in the 1990s was a strong feature of extra-curricular life, as well as a popular and successful Key Stage 3 course and GCSE option. *Getting On*, about the visit of a National Curriculum Inspector to a Welsh comprehensive in 1991 and the following year, *Margo's Guinevere*, in which the 1992 Bristol riots were interwoven with scenes from Arthurian England, were both ambitious but successful productions, written by the Head of Drama, Gareth Calway. The cast of *A Midsummer Night's Dream* in 1993 was dressed in 1960s hippy costumes and Howard Jones (1992-98) was a convincing teddy-boyish Bottom. He gave equally strong performances in Willy Russell's *Our Day Out*, June Shinn's first production as Head of Drama in 1994, and two years later in a highly entertaining musical play, *Big Al*, in which Howard was Al Capone. There was a large cast of nearly fifty and an excellent performance by Sara-Jane Brennock (1993-98) as the gangster's moll. The intervening year had seen a good production of *Macbeth*. Other successful productions followed, although there was not the usual school play in 1999/2000 because, along with two other high schools in Norfolk, K.E.S was invited to take part in a pageant of Norfolk life, past and present, at the Millennium Dome in March 2000. However, a performance of the pageant was also staged in the school hall. June Shinn's swansong in 2001 was a highly successful production of J B Priestley's *An Inspector Calls*. One of the stars of that play and also of *In Holland Stands a House* in 2002, a play about Anne Frank, which was expertly produced by Carol Beveridge, was Sophie Steer (1996-2003) who went on to read drama at university and embark on an acting career.

Towards the end of the 1980s music had gone through a low patch and, like Mr Greaves when he arrived, I had to create opportunities for more students to learn to play musical instruments so as to boost the size of the orchestra. By 1991/92 the number taking lessons had increased to fifty-four and there was both a senior and a junior orchestra. The Christmas Concert in December 1994 marked a significant turning point and, over the years, under the direction of the Head of Music, Chris Dixon, the orchestra, the wind band and the various ensembles became increasingly impressive both in numbers and in the standard of the music. The 1997 Christmas concert, for example, involved over 100 students and staff. By 1998/99 there were twenty K.E.S. musicians in the West Norfolk Jubilee Youth Orchestra or Wind Band, over a quarter of the members, despite the fact that they were drawn from all the West Norfolk high schools. Groups of K.E.S. musicians performed with increasing frequency at various public functions throughout the county.

There are many benefits to be gained from trips and visits, including travel abroad, and, certainly in the comprehensive era, the school saw them as an essential part of what it did to foster the social, cultural and intellectual development of the students. Many of the trips in the 1990s originated in the previous decade or even earlier. Some were lost but others took their place and the number and range of such trips increased. In 1990/91 some 150 students took part in the various trips organised by the Modern Languages Department, including the French and Spanish exchanges, the water-sports holiday to Anduze and the weekend trip to Dieppe. In 1993 the Brive exchange collapsed after running for thirty years and it proved difficult to find a new long-term partner.

The school hall in 1997 (M Walker/Lynn News)

The sports hall and gymnasium built in 1990/91 (M Walker/Norfolk County Council)

The Duke of York's visit to K.E.S. in 1991 (S Jukes/Lynn News)

Some of the newer buildings: the new teaching block and courtyard (1994); the Art/Technology block (1980); and the tennis clubhouse (2001) (M Walker/H Porter)

Top left: Learning to wind surf on an end-of-year activities day

Top right: Students on a Duke of Edinburgh Award expedition

Bottom left: A Year 9 mini-enterprise group

Bottom right: Funky Divas at the East of England Young Enterprise final at Churchill College, Cambridge (M. Walker)

A celebration cricket match, held to mark the John Smallwood's retirement in 1994 (Lynn News)

Students at work and play in the school year 2000/01. (M Walker)

Members of the Cricket tour to South Africa in 1997 (Lynn News)

The 2001 Year 11 Dinner (EDP)

The 1998 Gold Medal winner, Bridget Davies, receiving her award from the Queen (Lynn News)

The Queen unveiling a memorial plaque recording her visit in January 2007 (Lynn News)

The visit of the Queen in January 2007 (Lynn News)

To some extent this was because of changes in the organisation of French schools, in particular the division into 11-16 collèges and 16-19 lycées, since we wanted to send students from the 14-18 age range. However, there were successful exchanges to Chartres, Marseilles, Paris and Charroux, near Poitiers.

The popular sports tours and ski trips continued but went to more distant and more exciting destinations. There had been sports tours abroad in the 1980s and these continued with trips to Malta in 1994, to Holland in 1998, 2000 and 2002; and to Paris, also in 2000; but many tours continued to be in this country. However, the first of several ski trips to Canada and an under-15 cricket tour to South Africa, both in 1997, marked a new phase. The school believed it was the first state school to travel to South Africa for a cricket tour and the trip was a wonderful experience for those taking part, both students and staff. In order to help pay for the cost, various fund-raising events took place, including a dinner in the hall, at which the guest speaker was Old Lennensian Martin Brundle (1970-75), television commentator and former Formula One racing driver. Cricket tours to Barbados in 2000, 2002 and 2004 followed. The leadership of Paul Tebay as Director of Sport in the 1980s and 90s was outstanding.

Other school departments had organised trips in the past to the theatre, to art galleries, to conferences, to buildings and sites of historical interest and to carry out fieldwork. These continued but the programme expanded to include trips abroad. The Business Studies Department organised trips to Heidelberg in 1992 and Barcelona in 1996; there were Science trips to CERN, the European Centre for Nuclear Research, in 1994 and to Futuroscope, at Poitiers, in 2000; John Chappell, started what was to become a biennial trip to classical sites in Italy and Greece, with a trip to Rome, Pompeii and Herculaneum in 1998; and the History Department led a trip to the First World War battlefields in France also in 1998.

A major addition to the programme of trips came in the summer of 1991 when, for the first time, the last two days of the summer term were designated as Activities Days. This meant that the normal timetable was suspended and students were allowed to opt for a variety of activities and trips, including water-sports, dry-slope skiing, golf, fishing, cycling, go-karting and paint-balling. The aim was to end the year on a positive note rather than have it drift to a close.

The introduction of *Mini-enterprise Week* for Year 9 the following year also aimed to give a positive end to the summer term to a group which had completed SATs and chosen GCSE options for the following two years. For several years, each tutor group was divided up into companies to manufacture goods or devise services which would be sold at a trade fair at the end of the week. In 1996, for example, some 45 companies produced a wide range of goods including jewellery, paperweights, stress balls, cakes and home-made lemonade. Profits were donated to charity. Not only was the exercise one in which students developed a sense of business but it also fostered their team-working and inter-personal skills. The format changed at the end of the decade and from 2000 a three-day programme of activities was organised by the Norfolk Education, Industry and Commerce Group.

For members of Years 11 and 13 the end of year was marked by very popular formal dinners, followed by a disco for Year 11 and by a visit to a night club by the sixth formers. The Year 11 Dinner in particular was a wonderful opportunity for students to dress up and to attend, what was for many of them, their first formal meal and in the magnificent setting of the school hall. One of the keenly anticipated parts of the evening was how people would arrive at school. Taxis and stretch limos became the norm but more unusual modes of transport included motor bikes, a milk float and, for those really wanting to impress, a helicopter. The speech by the Head of Year relating incidents covering the five years he or she had been in charge of the group was always a cause of great hilarity and not a little embarrassment for some.

K.E.S. students were successful in a large number of different competitions in the 1990s. For example on two occasions, in 1990 and in 1994, teams of sixth formers won the Sedgewick Challenge, a general knowledge quiz broadcast on Radio Norfolk. On each occasion they won £750 for the school as well as individual prizes. Teams were regularly entered for Public Speaking competitions and in 1992 Billie Bartlem (1990-92), Emma Calow (1985-92) and Amanda Hopkins (1985-92) won through to the National Finals of the Business and Professional Women's Organisation competition in Glasgow. However it was in another general knowledge quiz, run on the same lines as television's *University Challenge*, that the school achieved national success. Having been beaten in the 1995 semi-final by the eventual winners, Lancaster Royal Grammar School, the 1996 team, Ben Ricketts (1994-2000), Theresa Brooks-Walker (1994-2001), Ian Dunn (1994-2001) and captain James Hayward (1995-2002) beat Dulwich College to become UK Junior Schools' Challenge Champions.

A different kind of success was that achieved by Chris Beanland (1991-98) in 1995, who received the Young Journalist of the Year Award from the British Heart Foundation and ASH (Action for Smoking and Health), for his excellent interviews and reports on under-age smoking for Channel 4's *Wise-Up* programme. In 1998 at the Norwich Science Olympiad at UEA, which involved over 550 students, the Year 9 and Year 10 teams both won Bronze Medals and the Year 8 team took the Rowntree Mackintosh Trophy for the best team in the age group. The school had success too in the sixth-form Young Enterprise competition, when the Funky Divas Company became the 2000 Norfolk Champions and won the Best Team Award in the East of England round at Churchill College, Cambridge, but narrowly missed winning through to the national finals. In the same year artwork submitted for the National Children's Art Competition won a prize of £1800 and a limited edition print of Anthony Gormley's *Destiny*. Staff and sixth-form students received the prize at a special Awards Ceremony in the Tate Modern a week before the official opening.

Many opportunities were offered to students outside the traditional range of extra-curricular activities. Sixth formers in particular were able to take part in a number of initiatives such as the Peer Drug Education and Peer Sex Education programmes. Others, from 1996, became involved as *Listeners*, a team of staff and students, led by Gordon Stone, which offered a friendly ear to anyone worried by problems at school or at home. The local branch of the Samaritans was involved each year in helping to train the *Listeners* and in 2000 two of the sixth formers, Jenny Diss (1994-2001) and Mark Fawkes (1994-2001), were invited to give a presentation about the K.E.S. scheme at the Samaritans' East of England Conference. This provoked such interest that they were then invited to speak at the National Conference at York later in the year, where they again had many requests for further information.

As in the 1980s, the PTA was very active, particularly in raising money for the school. In the 1990s social events continued to be a part of the annual programme, although very popular and well-attended quiz nights replaced dances as the main social get-togethers. The Summer Fete was the largest single fund-raiser in most years and it became a popular event for the younger students who were encouraged to have their own stalls. However, the most successful innovation was the Car Boot Sale, held three times a year from 1993. A dedicated band of parent volunteers established the K.E.S Car Boot Sales as the most successful in King's Lynn. The first one, in May 1993, raised

£850 but they went from strength to strength and by the end of the decade the profit from each one was over £2000. The school's position on the main road obviously helped but the boot sales were also extremely well run and both booters and buyers went away happy.

Another event put on by the PTA from 1993 was the welcome party in September for new parents. This was attended by all members of staff who taught Year 7 and was an opportunity for parents, not so much to discuss their children's progress as to meet staff and put faces to names. Obviously it also helped to alert staff to any difficulties being experienced by new students, although this seemed to be rare. The vast majority settled in quickly to the new routines and adjusted to being in a much bigger school; for many of them there were as many or more pupils in Year 7 as there had been in the whole of their primary or junior school.

The PTA contributed roughly £6000 per year to help pay for mini-buses, computers, a music laboratory, new equipment for the multi gym, a new sound system for the hall and drama staging. Very importantly, the PTA pledged £20,000 towards the £100,000 the school had to raise as part of the bid for Sports College Status. This was the largest single donation and without it the school would not have met its target.

Charity fund-raising was as a strong feature of the school as it had been since the early days when, for example, weekly collections were made for Belgian refugees in the autumn term of 1914 and for the *Red Cross* in the spring term of 1915. The school tried to foster a genuine concern for the less fortunate and parents were generous in supporting worthy causes. From early in the 1990s, rather than a school charity committee, each year group had a committee, which decided the particular charities it would support each year. For example in 1997, Year 11 raised over £1400 in a sponsored run, which went to the Children's Centre at the Queen Elizabeth Hospital; in 2000 Year 8 students handed over a cheque for £2180 to *Help the Aged*, although this included some money carried over from the previous year. Annual events in the fund-raising calendar included the Year 7 & 8 sponsored swim organised by the PE staff and the Year 7 Readathon run by the English Department. The latter, in 1999, raised some £1480 for *Sir Malcolm Sargent Cancer Care* and the *Roald Dahl Foundation*. Tragedies close to home often encouraged specific fund raising, for example £1100 from a sponsored walk led by Year 8 students was donated to various cancer charities after the sad death of twelve-year old Adam Blamire in September 1995. In addition, there were usually two or sometimes three non-uniform days each year to raise money for particular causes nominated by the school. In 2001/02, for example, £1200 was raised for *Amnesty International*, on the 25th Anniversary of the UN Declaration of Human Rights, £1032 for the *United Nations Children's Fund* and £1162 for the BBC's *Children in Need Appeal*. The overall amounts raised went up from about £3500 in 1990/91 to over £9000 per year at the turn of the century.

A number of staff retired in the period during which I was the Head. John Clubb, Gill Dyer and Ian Stockwell in 1990; Mike Wilkinson in 1991; Tony Hoey and David Smith in 1993; John Smallwood in 1994; Peter Hawkes in 1995; Richard Griffiths in 1996; Kate Wadlow in 1998; Heather Massen in 1999; Karin Price and June Shinn in 2001; Elizabeth Walker and Kitty Hall in 2002. Others moved on to well-deserved promotion. It would be invidious of me to comment on staff who are still at the school or who left relatively recently. There are so many people whose qualities I should like to praise. Almost certainly I should fail to mention someone who would be offended, and it would be unfair. Perhaps for the 125th anniversary in 2031 someone will write an update to this history by which time a more dispassionate view of the present staff will be possible. However, I make one exception, because it is quite clear that he is already a kind of legend. Mr J P Smallwood or 'Japes' as he has long been affectionately known is one of the best-loved characters of recent years. From comprehensive reorganisation in 1979 until he officially retired in 1994 after 35 years at the school, he was one of three Deputy Heads. He continued teaching archaeology (part-time) until 2001, when the new AS/A2 examinations replaced the old A levels. John also continued to manage one of the cricket teams. He made a massive contribution to cricket in the time he was at the school and generations of students benefited from his expertise and commitment. Mike Boagey (1959-66) says he was 'Certainly one of my favourites', a 1974 leaver Mark Buxton is similarly enthusiastic: 'What a star...Top man'; and Claire Sullivan, who left in 1995, says 'I cannot describe how much we loved this man!'

Reminiscences received from students who left in the recent past have been few. No doubt for the 125th anniversary they will be more prolific. As people get older they naturally become more interested in recalling past events including their schooldays. However one 2001 leaver has very happy memories of his time at K.E.S. Sam Chapman recalls with pleasure the 'relaxed and friendly atmosphere' that was allowed to develop in the upper school between teachers and students. On the odd occasion when he got into trouble, for example when he and some friends got drunk on the sixth form biology fieldtrip to Holt Hall, he appreciated the way he was treated by teachers whom he thought could have been much harsher. Looking back at his time at the school, Sam was surprised at 'how little bullying appeared to happen', despite the fact that he was, in his own words, 'a bit of a geek.' He also says that he never encountered drugs, 'which I suppose is quite amazing.' He suggests that may have been because of the people he associated with or because he was particularly unobservant, but goes on to say, 'You'd think I would have heard some gossip in seven years though!'

How successful was the school in the 1990s and early twenty first century? GCSE results at the beginning of the period were below both Norfolk and national averages but improved steadily if unevenly. In 1992, the first year of the publication of league tables, 51 students or 32.7% of the Year 11 cohort, gained five or more higher grades. However, two years later there was a significant breakthrough when 78 students (48.1%) achieved at least five A-C grades. Up to that year, only in 1988, the first year of GCSEs, was this number exceeded, and even then only by one. The results were also significantly higher than the average figures for Norfolk or for England as a whole and from 1994 this was to be the pattern. The best results at this level were in 1998 and 2001. In 1998, not only was the five higher-grades figure, at 62.7%, some 16 percentage points above the Norfolk and national averages, it came from the highest ever entry: 143 students out of a cohort of 228 achieved the benchmark. This was roughly double the number who gained five GCE 'O' levels in any year in the grammar school era. Another record was reached in 2001 when 136 out of 211, or 64.5%, achieve five or more A*-C grades. The most successful student in that year, Holly Wilkins (1996-2003), received letters of congratulation from the examination board for coming in the top five of all candidates in the country in both English Literature and in history. It was hardly surprising that two years later she gained five Grade As at GCE Advanced level and was the Gold Medallist.

At 'A' level, pass rates also rose from relatively low levels at the beginning of the 1990s. From 65.0% in 1990 and 72.2% in 1991 they jumped to 87.7% in 1992 and from then on there was almost a year-on-year improvement. The K.E.S. results were regularly the best or among the best in the fifty-two Norfolk LEA schools. In 2002 the pass rate had reached an impressive 96.7% and this was the fifth record year in a row. As well as the overall pass rate, the percentage of A and A, B or

C grades rose steadily. In 1991 the figures were 8% and 41.7% respectively but rose to 20% and 67% in 2002. The best top grade results were in 2000 when 88 of the 340 entries (26%) were As and 221 (65%) were A, B or C grades. The number of candidates in that year (99) was almost the highest ever to be entered by the school for 'A' level. Not surprisingly, in 2000 the school had 30 Norfolk Scholars. This was more than twice the then record number of 14 in 1973 in the heyday of the grammar school. There were some spectacular individual results in most years, for example, in 2000 Peter Steward (1993-2000) gained five A grades and received a letter of congratulation from the examination board for coming among the top five candidates in psychology. The following year Joanne Mullender (1994-2001), also gained five grade As and a letter of congratulation for her result in biology. She gained 594 marks (out of a maximum 600) on the six modules in the AS and A2 examinations. Both Peter and Joanne were Gold Medallists.

As mentioned in previous chapters, the K.E.S. Gold medal is normally presented by HM The Queen at Sandringham House in the New Year. The Head accompanies the successful student and they have a private audience for fifteen minutes or so during which time Her Majesty asks about the student's interests, experience of university life or gap year activities and chats about recent events. The students are inevitably nervous at the prospect of meeting the Queen but she very quickly puts them at their ease and each one whom I accompanied over the twelve years I was the Head found the audience a most enjoyable experience. Queen Elizabeth has already awarded over sixty Gold Medals, more than any of her predecessors, even Edward Vll. She has seen three Head Masters retire and perhaps has wondered at their lack of stamina compared with herself.

The Queen ensures that the presentation is made on a date convenient for the gold medal winner, usually before he or she is due to go back to university after Christmas. The presentation to the 2000 winner was held in December rather than in January 2001 because Peter Steward, who was having a gap year, was flying off to Africa just after Christmas. It could not have been a particularly convenient time as the members of the Royal Family were still arriving for the holiday and I remember seeing the late Queen Mother's trunks being unloaded while we were there.

At no other state secondary school is a Gold Medal awarded by the Queen for academic achievement. In fact very few schools have such an award. Apart from military and naval colleges, only Winchester and Wellington Colleges and Rugby School are honoured in this way. There is a parallel prize, a leather-bound book, for example, of the complete works of Shakespeare, awarded to the best student at Springwood High School in King's Lynn. This prize was first presented in 1888 to a student at the King's Lynn High School for Girls by the then Princess of Wales. As Queen Alexandra she continued the presentation until her death, after which the tradition was maintained first by Queen Mary and then by Queen Elizabeth, the Queen Mother. Since 2003, it has been awarded by the Queen.

Most of the Gold Medal winners have inevitably been boys as the school was single-sex until 1979. The first girl was Nina Constable in 1993. A small number of gold medal winners have been the sons of staff at the school: John Vernon (1951), the son of Leslie Vernon, Deputy Head from 1959 to 69; Michael Seaman (1974) whose father, Bryan, was Head of Chemistry; Daniel Griffiths (1982), son of Richard Griffiths, Deputy Head from 1973 to 1996; my son, Andrew Walker, (2002); and Ben Osborne (2005), son of Andy Osborne, Deputy Head, 1994 to 2014.

In two successive years K.E.S. teachers were awarded prizes. For improvements in the GSCE results over the three years to 2000 and for the excellence of the 2001 results the school received special grants of £32,760 and £34,000 respectively, which were distributed to teaching and non-teaching staff. These school Achievement Awards have since been discontinued.

The Ofsted inspections in 1995 and 2000 both praised the school. That in 1995 was the first full inspection since 1957. The main findings of the report were that the school was efficiently run and had 'many good and some outstanding features.' The report said that the school was going through a period of change and improvement and most of the areas where further development was needed had already been identified as priorities. One of the features of the school which the report picked out for particular praise was 'the programme of training and supervision of newly qualified teachers,' organised by Staff Development Co-ordinator, Mrs Kitty Hall, which was described as 'exemplary.' The inspectors might have added that this was also true of the work done with PGCE students from Cambridge. The school had been a principal cluster school, linked to the Cambridge Department of Education and Homerton College since September 1994. In addition, PE students from De Montfort University (Bedford College) were also placed at K.E.S. for teaching practice because of the high standard of supervision.

Because the school came out well in 1995 it was selected for one of the new short inspections in 2000 and this was even more complimentary. The report of that inspection concluded:

> 'This is a very effective school in almost all respects. It achieves high standards overall, but could do better for older, low-attaining pupils. Teaching is very good. Very effective leadership and high expectations create a purposeful, happy, orderly school that has high achievement at its heart and seeks to improve further. It gives very good value for money.'

As a result of this inspection the school was listed in the Annual Report of the Chief Inspector of Schools for 1999/2000 as 'particularly successful.' Along with Heads of secondary schools named in that and other reports I was invited to a special reception given by the Prince of Wales at his Gloucestershire home, Highgrove House, in May 2002, as an acknowledgement of the work being done to raise standards. The invitation was made to 'Heads of secondary schools known for the excellence which they represent and for the contribution they make to the highest standards of teaching.'

A further acknowledgment of the school's success came in March 2002 when the London University Institute of Education published the results of research entitled *Establishing the Current State of School Leadership in England*. Ten schools were used as case studies and one of the four secondary schools chosen to illustrate good practice was King Edward Vll School. One of the statements made is that 'The school enjoys immense prestige in the locality and is oversubscribed every year... Estate agents use the location of a house in the school's catchment area as a positive selling point.' Clearly the school was seen by parents as successful, since from 1992 there were consistently more applications than places and independent panels met regularly to consider appeals by parents for admission. In 1999, for example, there were over 300 applications for the 219 places. The roll increased from 1063 in 1991 to over 1300 by 1997 and the school tried to limit further growth believing that any further increase would reduce its effectiveness.

In 2002 the school entered a new phase in its development with the appointment of Mr M J Douglass as Head. Mike Douglass joined the school as a Deputy Head in 1996 on the retirement of Richard Griffiths. He had been Head of Humanities in a very large Essex comprehensive and soon made his mark in the school as the Deputy overseeing the pastoral system, special needs and primary liaison. In later years he had responsibility for the timetable and curriculum, for staff welfare, and a whole range of administrative tasks. One of his great strengths was his inter-personal

Michael Douglass, Head from 2002 to 2014

skills and he was responsible for securing Investors in People status for the school. Indeed in all aspects of his work as a Deputy Head he showed expertise and effectiveness of the highest order and it was not surprising that the Governors chose him to succeed me in 2002.

It is not my intention to write in any detail about the period following my retirement in 2002. That must be left for a future publication. However I should like to mention just a few examples which indicate that the school's success is ongoing. In athletics, for example, in 2004 Lewis Ely, in Year 11, returned from the British Blind Athletic Championships at Nuneaton in Warwickshire in November with three Gold Medals and two British records. Lewis, who is partially sighted, won the 100m in a record time of 13.3 seconds and jumped 1.7 m to break the High Jump record, as well as bringing home a third Gold in the Discus competition.

For many years the school has involved large numbers of students in leadership and community service programmes and several of them have won prizes recognising their achievements. As already mentioned, four K.E.S. students were fortunate to accompany the British team to the Winter Olympics in 2002. A year later, sixth former James Crawley was one of four students selected, at the annual camp for Millennium Volunteers at Loughborough University, to attend the Hampden Academy in Maine for a week's course. And at a similar camp in March 2004 for the newly-named Step into Sport Community Volunteers, Lizzy Barnes, in Year 12, was selected, as one of only four students (two boys and two girls) from over 400 young people, to attend the Youth Olympic Challenge in Athens (12-23 August). Like those who went to the Winter Olympics in 2002 she had a wonderful time, meeting the UK athletes, attending some of the events and seeing the sights of the Greek capital.

A word too about a success in public speaking which has long been a key aspect of the school's extra-curricular programme. In 2005 Sarah Tranter, Janaka Sasitharan and Ester Press, as East of England Champions, won through to the national final of the Business and Professional Women's competition at Oswestry. They were a credit to themselves and the school and worthy runners up to the winning team from Northern Ireland.

Finally I must give an account of some of the events which occurred after the publication of the first edition of this book in 2005 which had been produced in anticipation of the centenary of the opening of the building on the Gaywood Road by King Edward VII.

The approaching centenary led to a revival of interest in the history of the school and in the Old Lennensians' Association (OLA) which had been wound up in the early 1980s. At a meeting held on 2 November 2005 it was decided to re-form the association. A new constitution was agreed upon and John Turtle was elected Chairman, John Marsters, Vice Chairman, Don Oliver, Secretary and David Cobbold, Treasurer. Judge Peter Jacobs was invited to be the President. One of the first tasks of the new committee was to plan a grand re-union dinner to celebrate the centenary of the opening of the school on the Gaywood Road. The interest was so great that in the event two dinners were held, one at Leziate Park Country Club and the other at Isle College in Wisbech. At the first, the guest speakers were William Lancaster, great-grandson of the benefactor of the school, and Paul Bromhead, whose father Tom had taught at the school from 1921 to 1955. At the other dinner Peter Jacobs and John Sleigh spoke eloquently of their time as pupils and John was able to give an insight into his father's time as Head Master for 25 years. These events were masterminded by David Cobbold.

Andrew Stephen

In the years since then the OLA has been very active. Each year there have been annual re-unions as well as other get-togethers and the association has given the school significant financial support for a number of projects. In 2018 many of the original members of the committee indicated their intention to resign but under the enthusiastic Chairmanship of Andrew Stephen (1964-71) a new committee was elected at the AGM in June to take the association forward. However, to recognise the contribution made by the former committee members, they were all appointed Vice Presidents of the association. There are currently over 240 members but the great majority are from the days of the Boys' Grammar School. One important aim for the future is to increase membership from students of the comprehensive era.

The major event celebrating the centenary was the visit by Her Majesty Queen Elizabeth II on 24 January 2007. As described in Chapter 5 she had helped the school to celebrate its fiftieth anniversary by her visit in 1956 and fifty years on she honoured the school once again. After a welcome by civic dignitaries and the Chairman of Governors, Mrs Tess Gilder, the Head, Michael Douglass, invited the Queen to unveil a stone plaque near to the statue of Edward VII to commemorate her visit. Large numbers of excited pupils on the forecourt had the opportunity to see the Queen's arrival and the unveiling ceremony. Unlike fifty years previously no tour of the school was planned. Instead the Queen was introduced to a number of representative groups in the school hall:

Group 1. Staff of Norfolk Children's Services, Property Services and Mansell Construction Company. The latter was the contractor for a new six-classroom block due to be completed in the summer of 2007.

Group 2. Representatives of the 98 teaching and 50 non-teaching staff.

Group 3. A group of former pupils: members the Old Lennensians' Association, including Judge Peter Jacobs, John Turtle and John Sleigh; and three Gold Medal winners from the early 2000s: Andrew Walker, Holly Wilkins, and Ben Osborne.

Group 4. Young Ambassadors, Millennium Volunteers, CSLA and JSLA students who were introduced to Her Majesty by Paul Tebay, Director of Sport.

Group 5. Duke of Edinburgh Award candidates at Bronze, Silver and Gold levels.

Group 6. The Head Boy and Head Girl as well as students representing each year.

At the time the school had an educational link with China and there were a number of Chinese guests in the hall who were also presented to the Queen.

With all these groups, members of the senior staff and/or governors were present to effect introductions or give explanations. The visit was organised brilliantly by the Head so as to include as many people as possible while representing all aspects of school life.

As in previous decades, former K.E.S. students from the 1990s and 2000s have been successful in a wide range of professions – in accountancy, education, information technology, law, medicine, science and engineering, to name but a few. Many are also making very positive contributions to the life of King's Lynn and West Norfolk in a variety of occupations. One alumna who has already become well known on the national scene is Lucy Verasamy who left school in 1998. She became a presenter on *ITV Weather* in 2012, since 2017 has also been part of the ITV Racing team and in August 2018 she joined *Good Morning Britain* as a relief weather presenter.

This book has traced the important part played by King Edward Vll School in the education of young people from King's Lynn and beyond over the past century and earlier. Students and staff, past and present, can be very proud of their association with a school which has enriched the lives of generations of young people in so many ways.

Crescat in horas doctrina

Appendices

(a) K.E.S. Gold Medal Winners

1864	H B Bristow	1918	E Goodbody	1969	C J Steward
1865	A E Flaxman	1919	W W Grave	1970	D Rix
1866	A E Flaxman	1920	P H N Palmer	1971	P T Such
1867	W Hoff	1921	J W Smith	1972	R L A Goodings
1868	A B Howard	1922	J A F Shipp	1973	J E Robbs
1869	R R Harper	1923	G J Jary	1974	M J Seaman
1870	A Cornish	1924	D R Bunn	1975	M D Stafford
1871	R L Collier	1925	E D Munford	1976	T R Holland
1872	H W Cornish	1926	G G Dorer	1977	P I H Cooke
1873	H Leeper	1927	G A Way	1978	M A Fuller
1874/75	F C Davis	1928	P G Seapey	1979	J M Holmes
1875/76	E Hall	1929	P H Lenton	1980	P A Hall
1876/77	W H Bennell	1930	G D Anderson	1981	N A C Holman
1877/78	E A Fitch	1931	A V E J Mindham	1982	D R L Griffiths
1878/79	H H Leeper	1932	R T R Thornhill	1983	R J Dowling
1879/80	J W Court	1933	E G Bales	1984	P M Jones
1880/81	G A Mossop	1934	G T Langley	1985	M A Schumann
1881/82	E E Hitchcock	1935	E F Thurston	1986	S Chakraborti
1882/83	F E Suckling	1936	R N A Smith	1987	J P Green
1883/84	W F Swann	1937	E W M Hamilton	1988	S King
1885	O F Pilling	1938	D Fysh	1989	N Iyengar
1886	A T Tallent	1939	B S Hayward	1990	C N Mills
1889	A Swann	1940	J A Thurston	1991	G E Hart
1890	E P Barrett	1941	E J Horsford	1992	P M Rendell
1891	G B E Riddell	1942	J J Wilkins	1993	Nina R Constable
1892	J D Coe	1943	D W Collins	1994	D R Meek
1893	F W Thompson	1944	L D G Hamilton	1995	M P Welberry Smith
1894	A R Firth	1945	B K Blenkinsop	1996	Tabitha J Cooper
1895	P H Winfield	1946	J H Young	1997	S Fukes
1896	F G Firth	1947	J A Greeves	1998	Bridget C Davies
1897	H G Lemmon	1948	T R W Hampton	1999	N J Tebbutt
1898	G F Middleton	1949	R E Whiley	2000	P R Steward
1899	W D Keyworth	1950	R B Arnold	2001	Joanne L Mullender
1900	E N H May	1951	J F Vernon	2002	A M N Walker
1901	H L Morgan	1952	P F T Linford	2003	Holly A Wilkins
1902	H Firth	1953	G M Hamilton	2004	Frances M Piggott
1903	F W Dudding	1954	A B Crowfoot	2005	B I Osborne
1904	G R Mines	1955	C W Smith	2006	C J L Vingoe
1905	P G Bales	1956	R H Gathercole	2007	Kathryn Lee
1906	B H Binks	1957	R P Hanage	2008	L Atkinson
1907	R H Tilson	1958	B G Eke	2009	R May
1908	P K Lockwood	1959	R S Peckover	2010	Alexandra Rutterford
1909	F S Shears	1960	M J G Lee	2011	T Clark
1910	R G Metcalf	1961	G J Fayers	2012	A P Cole
1911	C L McKenzie	1962	D M Shotton	2013	Xuesong Wu
1912	R G Ruscoe	1963	B H Collison	2014	Z Tham
1913	S Brook	1964	R J Shipp	2015	Hannah Hodges
1914	H S Raby	1965	M H Smith	2016	S M Lott
1915	H A Scott	1966	R E Halliwell	2017	O Dewey
1916	T M Edmunds	1967	S J Sauvain	2018	C Micu
1917	H E Howard	1968	J C Gore		

(b) K.E.S. School Captains 1919 - 1985

1919	W W Grave	1942	F F Silk	1964/65	J Barrett
1920	J A F Shipp	1943	LD G Hamilton	1965	A J Williams
1921	J A F Shipp	1944	G L Butcher	1966	A J L Huns
1922	E M Dimmock	1945	F C Cresey	1966	D R Rout
1923	N E H Watson	1946	A J Shepard	1966/67	J M Sharpe
1924	C M Bayfield	1947	A J Shepard	1967/68	P B Roscoe
1925	C M Bayfield	1948	R E Lack	1968/69	D A Jackson
1926	G G Dorer	1949	P M T Banyard	1969	P J M Hollingworth
1927	G A Way	1950	R E Whiley	1969/70	S G Collison
1928	G A Way	1951	P A Sauvain	1970/71	J Rye
1929	D E Macey	1951/52	S R Coltman	1971/72	M A G McDonnell
1930	T N V C Rose-Price	1952/53	G M Hamilton	1972/73	G J Belham
1931	H Eggleton	1953/54	P D Bromhead	1973/74	P R Hall
1931	W G Wright	1954	A B Crowfoot	1974/75	M J Watson
1932	H E Hargrave	1955	M R Begley	1975/76	S R Fretwell
		1956	D Fleming	1976/77	C P Hall
1934	G T Langley	1956/57	D W Pearman	1977/78	D Wright
1935	D H Drennan	1957/58	R E A Butler	1978/79	A J Russell
1936	J K Wagstaff	1958/59	B G Eke	1979/80	P A Hall
1937	E W M Hamilton	1959/60	A E Tovell	1980/81	P R Lemon
1938	D Fysh	1960	G R Bretten	1981/82	M J Smith
1939	B S Hayward	1961	R S Peckover	1982/83	R Andrew
1940	L B Bell	1961-63	R C Goat	1983/84	R W Brain
1940	A J Porter	1963	A V Bland	1984/85	D J Grint
1941	W A Baillie	1963/64	D Wayre		

(c) K.E.S. Head Boys and Head Girls 1985 - 2018

1985/86	Andrew Woods / Nicola Clemens	1996/97	James Crockett / Kelly Pattison	2007/08	Solomon Prestidge / Alice Coe
1986/87	Etuka Onono / Sally Small	1997/98	Richard Pearce / Emma Watson	2008/09	Christopher Claxton-Shirley / Emma Cave
1987/88	John Truman / Nicola Jameson	1998/99	Christopher Hodson / Natalie Smith	2009/10	Kieran Bunting / Alex Rutterford
1988/89	Matthew Brooksbank / Emily Daniell	1999/2000	David Jamieson / Susannah Barrett	2010/11	Joshua Green / Francesca Walder
1989/90	Matthew Shaw / Catherine Haynes	2000/01	Allister Hodson / Theresa Walker	2011/12	James Marsh / Emily Nolan
1990/91	William Bond / Katy Rose	2001/02	Timothy Calloway / Sally Little	2012/13	Jack Twyman / Florence Mather
1991/92	Andrew Daly / Emma Calow	2002/03	Michael Culham / Sophie Steer	2013/14	Joshua Jackson / Holly Myers
1992/93	Alison Brockhurst / Michael Rudd	2003/04	Robin Foster / Rachel Eyre	2014/15	Thomas Pipkin / Ilaria Pezzella
1993/94	Samuel Healey / Amanda Walker	2004/05	Jaimin Thakrar / Janaka Sasitharan	2015/16	Lukas Petraska / Molly Hemeter
1994/95	Matthew Welberry Smith / Nichola Kentzer	2005/06	William Parry / Kayleigh Kew	2016/17	Karl Brown / Belinda Clark
1995/96	David Martin / Emma Hately	2006/07	Thomas Mulready / Gemma Beal	2017/18	James Wharf / Kate Sycamore

(d) The 1972 whole-school photograph

The 1972 whole-school photograph (1)

The 1972 whole-school photograph (2)

The 1972 whole-school photograph (3)

The 1972 whole-school photograph (4)

137

The 1972 whole-school photograph (5)

Index